Whispers of the Arcane

How to Become a Wizard

Part of the "A Journey into the World of" series
by Norman Creek Press

Edited by Tuan MacCairillyn

Whispers of the Arcane: How to Become a Wizard
Copyright © 2023 Norman Creek Press

All rights reserved. No part of this book may be reproduced or transmitted in any form or by any means without written permission from the author.

ISBN (XXXXXXXXXXXX)

Whispers of the Arcane: How to Become a Wizard is the first book in Norman Creek Press's 'Journey into the World of' series.

This book is recommended for mature audiences (M15+).

Dedication

To all the aspiring wizards, enchanters, and spellcasters,

This book is dedicated to you, the curious souls who yearn to unlock the secrets of the mystical arts. To those who have longed to be the next Merlin, Gandalf, or Hermione (or maybe even a combination of all three, because who doesn't love a good mashup?), this book is here to fuel your magical ambitions. Grab your robes, don your pointy hat, and prepare to dive headfirst into a world where potions bubble, cauldrons brew, and broomsticks occasionally double as unreliable means of transportation.

But let's not forget another set of intrepid souls who deserve a shoutout. To all those with a boundless curiosity about the natural world, this dedication is extended to you as well. Because let's face it, who needs magic when reality itself is filled with wonders beyond imagination? From the peculiar quirks of quantum physics to the mesmerizing dance of fireflies on a summer night, nature's enchantment knows no bounds.

So, whether you're wielding a wand or dissecting a dandelion, remember to embrace the magic of the universe with a pinch of humor. And if things go awry, don't fret! Even the greatest wizards have occasionally turned their eyebrows into fluffy caterpillars or conjured up dancing broomsticks that refuse to sit still.

In the spirit of laughter and discovery, may this book be your companion on a whimsical journey where magic and the natural world collide. May it inspire you to pursue your wizarding dreams while reminding you to cherish the mysteries that unfold right beneath our noses.

Table of Contents

Foreword 5

Preface 6

Introduction – The Enchanted Chronicles 8

Chapter 1 The Enigma of Wizards 14

Chapter 2 Merlin the Arch-Druid............................. 19

Chapter 3 Odin and the Magical Runes 23

Chapter 4 Gender-Diverse Wizards 27

Chapter 5 Baba Yaga the Guardian of Mysteries.... 34

Chapter 6 Amara the Wise 38

Chapter 7 Chinese Alchemy and Mysticism 42

Chapter 8 Indian Wizards and Yogis 46

Chapter 9 Magic in the Americas 51

Chapter 10 High and Low Magic 58

Chapter 11 Indigenous Magic 66

Chapter 12 Black, White, and Gray Magic 73

Chapter 13 Magic of Different Colors 77

Chapter 14 Ceremonial Magic................................ 80

Chapter 15 Right-hand Path vs. Left-hand Path...... 85

Chapter 16 Skeptics and Frauds 88

Chapter 17 The Wisdom of Wizards....................... 91

Chapter 18 Setting Up Shop 93

Afterword 98

Foreword

In the dim-lit corners of the world, where shadows twist and secrets lurk, there exists a realm hidden from mortal eyes. A realm where arcane forces converge, and the timeless art of wizardry weaves its gossamer web. It is in this mystic world that this grimoire has ventured, delving deep into the annals of history and society to illuminate the enigmatic path of the wizard.

In this tome, aptly titled "Whispers of the Arcane: How to Become a Wizard," This book expounds an extraordinary chronicle that enthralls and enchants, revealing the hidden secrets of a veiled realm and giving real-world advice about how to become a wizard. As an inquisitive observer, it undertakes the daunting task of unraveling the mysteries surrounding those who delve into the powers beyond the veil.

This tome embarks upon a voyage through the ages, tracing the elusive footprints of wizards, searching a labyrinth of ancient beliefs, and unlocking caskets of knowledge acquired by experience and research. In these pages, the tenebrous corners of wizardry's world are illuminated.

As the reader turns each page, they will be transported to a world where reality intertwines with the ethereal, where the past is ever-present, and the unknown beckons. Its words weave a spell of their own, captivating the mind and stirring the imagination, inviting us to peer behind the veil and answering the question of how we too might become a wizard.

Preface

Welcome to the captivating world of wizardry, where ancient spells intertwine with mystic forces, and the arcane arts shape the fabric of reality. Within these pages, you will embark on an extraordinary journey into the realm of magic, where imagination and opportunity know no bounds. This book, born out of a fascination for the subject, aims to illuminate the wonders of wizardry and unveil the secrets that lie hidden within the annals of fantasy and mythology, offering advice on how people with such an inclination could take their place in their community as the local wizard.

From the very beginning, humans have been enchanted by tales of sorcery and the enigmatic figures who wielded its power. From the spellbinding wizards of ancient Mesopotamia to the mythical Merlin of Arthurian legend, the concept of magic has ignited the collective imagination across cultures and civilizations. The allure of sorcery has transcended time and permeated the realms of literature, art, and folklore, capturing the hearts and minds of countless individuals throughout history.

The genesis of this book can be traced back to a shared passion for all things magical and otherworldly. Our quest to understand the essence of wizardry has led us down a winding path of research, delving into ancient tomes and exploring the rich tapestry of legends and folklore from around the globe.

During our exploration, we encountered extraordinary tales of wizards who harnessed the forces of nature, shaped destinies and transcended the limits of mortal existence. Their stories, woven through time, are like gossamer threads that connect us to a realm where the impossible becomes possible, and where the boundaries of reality blur with the ethereal.

With this book, we endeavor to bring forth the essence of wizardry, drawing upon a multitude of sources, including ancient texts, epic sagas, and the collective wisdom of countless cultures. From the ancient spellcraft of Egyptian sorcerers to the arcane rituals of Celtic druids, we seek to provide a comprehensive exploration of the diverse traditions and practices that have shaped the concept of wizardry.

As you embark on this journey, prepare to be enthralled by tales of the intricate workings of magical arts. Delve into the intricacies of spellcasting, potion brewing, and the profound philosophies that underpin the wizard's craft. Uncover the extraordinary powers of the mind and the mastery of arcane symbols that allow the wizard to manipulate the very fabric of reality.

While this book serves as a compendium of knowledge, it is also an invitation for you, the reader, to awaken your own inner wizard. Let the wisdom contained within these pages inspire your imagination and kindle the spark of magic that resides within your own being. May you find solace in the world of wizardry, where the fantastical and the mundane intertwine, and where the boundaries of possibility are limited only by the scope of your imagination.

So, turn the page and step into a realm where the extraordinary becomes ordinary, and the mysteries of wizardry unfold before your eyes. Welcome to a world where reality and enchantment converge—the world of wizardry.

Introduction – The Enchanted Chronicles

In the realm of mysticism and wonder, where arcane forces intertwine with the fabric of reality, a world of extraordinary beings exists. Among them, the enigmatic figures known as wizards stand as luminous pillars of ancient wisdom and formidable power. Welcome to The Enchanted Chronicles, an enthralling exploration into the realms of wizardry and the remarkable individuals who have wielded its mystical forces throughout history.

From the ancient lands of Egypt, Mesopotamia, China, Asia, and Persia, tales of formidable wizards echo through the annals of time. In Egypt, the sorcerer-priests invoked incantations and tapped into the power of the gods, wielding magic as an extension of divine will. Meanwhile, Mesopotamian sorcerers inscribed their spells upon clay tablets, summoning spirits and influencing the forces of nature.

In the Far East, China and Asia witnessed the rise of masterful practitioners of wizardry. The sages of China's Taoist traditions immersed themselves in meditation and alchemy, cultivating their inner energies to shape the world around them. Across the vast expanse of Asia, mystics and shamanic figures tapped into the primal forces of nature, invoking spirits, and channeling their energy for the betterment of their communities.

The ancient Persian empire bore witness to sorcerers who communed with demons, using their unearthly knowledge to manipulate events and weave intricate webs of power. Their practices blended mysticism and religion, creating magical rituals and incantations.

Throughout history, tales of wizards have been intertwined with the extraordinary powers they wield. From the ability to manipulate the elements to divination and shapeshifting, the powers ascribed to these enigmatic figures have fascinated and captivated generations. Some claimed wizards could bend reality to their will, heal the sick with a single touch, or traverse vast distances in an instant. Others were said to command the celestial bodies, unlock hidden knowledge, or even resurrect the dead.

To understand the essence of wizardry, one must first comprehend what it means to be a wizard. In its purest form, a wizard is an individual who has harnessed and mastered the secrets of magic—a conduit between the physical and the ethereal. They are seekers of esoteric knowledge, delving into the depths of the unknown to acquire wisdom that extends beyond mortal comprehension.

There are several terms used to describe various magic users from literature and legend, and it may be of some use to understand the differences between them:

Wizard: A wizard is a skilled practitioner of magic, often depicted as having extensive knowledge and mastery over various spells and arcane arts. Wizards are typically associated with intelligence, study, and the casting of spells through incantations and gestures. This tome will mainly focus on wizards and how to become one.

Witch: A witch is a practitioner of magic, usually depicted as female, who is often associated with nature, herbalism, and casting spells. In folklore and mythology, witches are often portrayed as having supernatural powers and abilities. Men can be witches too, and Wicca has become very popular these days. However, wizards are emphatically not witches. Their path is different in many obvious and subtle ways.

Warlock: A warlock is a male practitioner of magic. The term is often used to refer to a sorcerer or magician who has made a pact with supernatural beings or dark forces to gain power. In some contexts, "warlock" may have negative connotations, suggesting a practitioner of black magic. Wizards are not warlocks, a warlock is a term more frequently used for a male witch, although, as mentioned, it does have a negative connotation.

Necromancer: A necromancer is a practitioner of necromancy, a form of magic that involves communicating with or manipulating the spirits of the dead. Necromancers are often associated with dark and forbidden arts, as well as the ability to raise and control the undead. This tome does not recommend dabbling in the dark arts.

Sorcerer: A sorcerer is a practitioner of sorcery, a type of magic that is typically derived from innate talent or bloodline. Sorcerers often possess inherent magical abilities and can cast spells without relying heavily on study or formal training.

Enchanter: An enchanter is a magic user who specializes in casting enchantments and charms. Enchanters can imbue objects or people with magical properties or to create illusions.

Conjurer: A conjurer is a magic user who specializes in conjuring or summoning objects, creatures, or forces from other realms or dimensions. Conjurers often employ rituals or spells to bring forth their desired entities or phenomena.

Polymorph: Polymorph refers to the magical ability to change one's form or shape. A polymorph spell or ability allows the caster to transform themselves or others into different creatures or objects temporarily.

Abjurer: An abjurer is a magic user who specializes in protective or defensive magic. Abjurers are skilled at creating barriers, shields, and wards to repel or neutralize magical threats or spells.

Illusionist: An illusionist is a magic user who specializes in creating illusions or false perceptions. Illusionists can cast spells or use their abilities to manipulate light, sound, and other senses, creating convincing and deceptive illusions.

Summoner: A summoner is a magic user who can summon or call forth creatures or entities from other planes of existence. Summoners often form contracts or pacts with these beings to lend their aid or to be controlled by the summoner. This text does not recommend this sort of magic.

Druid: A druid is a magic user who is deeply connected to nature and its forces. Druids often can communicate with animals, control the elements, and perform rituals to heal or protect the natural world.

Hierophant: A hierophant is a religious or mystical figure who holds sacred knowledge and acts as an interpreter or mediator between the divine and mortal realms. Hierophants are often associated with rituals, ceremonies, and the teaching of esoteric wisdom.

Pythoness: A pythoness, also known as a Pythia or oracle, is a female prophet or seer who is believed to have the ability to communicate with the gods or divine entities. In ancient Greece, the most famous pythoness was the Oracle of Delphi, who delivered prophecies and advice to seekers.

Alchemist: An alchemist is an individual who practices alchemy, a philosophical and proto-scientific tradition that emerged in the ancient world. Alchemists were known for their pursuits in transforming base metals into noble metals like gold and for seeking the elixir of life, which was believed to grant immortality. They also delved into mystical and spiritual aspects, such as exploring the connection between the physical and spiritual realms. Alchemists often worked with various substances and symbols to perform experiments and rituals aimed at achieving their goals.

Ceremonial Magician: A ceremonial magician is an individual who practices a specific type of magic characterized by elaborate rituals and ceremonial practices. These rituals often involve the use of symbols, tools, and invocations to access and manipulate supernatural forces or entities. Ceremonial magicians may follow systems like Hermeticism, Kabbalah, or the Golden Dawn, and they often study grimoires and ancient texts to gain knowledge and power. The practice of ceremonial magic typically focuses on personal transformation, spiritual growth, and the exploration of the divine.

Wu: In Chinese culture, a "Wu" refers to a shaman or spiritual practitioner who acts as an intermediary between the human world and the spirit realm. Wu are believed to possess the ability to communicate with spirits, deities, and ancestors, and they use this connection to provide guidance, healing, and divination for their community. Wu often perform rituals, make offerings, and use various tools like drums, incense, and talismans in their practice. They hold a respected role within Chinese society and are consulted for matters related to health, fortune, and spiritual matters.

Shukenja: In the context of Japanese culture, a shukenja is a type of cleric or priest who combines both religious and magical practices. Shukenja are typically associated with Shintoism and Buddhism and may serve as intermediaries between the divine and the human world. They perform religious ceremonies, offer prayers, and provide spiritual guidance to their communities. Shukenja may also possess knowledge and skills in magical arts like healing, exorcism, and divination, which they use to address physical, emotional, and spiritual ailments.

Sage: A sage is an individual who is highly regarded for their wisdom, knowledge, and insight. Sages are often recognized for their deep understanding of the human condition, the natural world, or spiritual truths. They may have accumulated their wisdom through years of study, personal experiences, or a deep connection with the divine. Sages are often sought out for guidance, mentorship, and their ability to provide profound insights into complex matters. In various cultures and traditions, sages are revered figures who hold significant influence and respect.

Shaman: A shaman is a spiritual practitioner who is believed to have the ability to interact with the spirit world on behalf of their community. Shamans are found in many indigenous cultures around the world and play vital roles in healing, divination, spiritual guidance, and maintaining a balance between the physical and spiritual realms. They often undergo rigorous training and may use techniques like trance states, rituals, and the use of herbs or sacred objects to connect with spirits and perform their duties. Shamans are seen as mediators between the human and spirit realms and often possess unique abilities to navigate and influence these realms.

Like any force in the universe, the powers of wizardry possess the capacity for both benevolence and malevolence. Throughout the ages, wizards have walked divergent paths, with some harnessing their abilities for the greater good, while others succumb to darkness and use their powers to sow chaos and destruction. Good wizards, often known as enchanters or sages, become guardians of wisdom and defenders of justice. In contrast, their malevolent counterparts, dark sorcerers, or necromancers, embrace the shadows and seek dominion overall.

Join us as we embark on a captivating journey through the annals of wizardry, delving into the tales of extraordinary beings and their magical exploits. From the ancient civilizations to the far corners of the world, let us unlock the secrets of wizardry, peer into the depths of their powers, and unravel the mystery of wizardry that has fascinated humanity since time immemorial.

Chapter One - The Enigma of Wizards

"Magic is not a miracle. It is a science." - Baba Hari Dass

"Every great wizard in history has started out as nothing more than what we are now: students. If they can do it, why not us?" - J.K. Rowling

"Wizardry is the art of harnessing the unseen forces of the universe to shape reality." – Merlin

Wizards, the arcane and exotic figures of human imagination, have fascinated us throughout history and literature. Their mysterious powers and ability to manipulate the world around them have captured the minds of generations. This chapter delves into the profound question: What is a wizard? By examining the nature of wizardry and exploring the lives of famous historical and fictional wizards, we aim to unravel the intricacies of this remarkable phenomenon.

Defining a Wizard: A wizard can be defined as an individual who possesses exceptional knowledge and mastery over arcane arts, employing their skills to manifest supernatural abilities and manipulate the fabric of reality. Wizards often engage in the practice of wizardry, an ancient discipline rooted in the understanding and manipulation of mystical energies and forces. These practitioners channel their understanding of the unseen to achieve remarkable feats beyond the comprehension of ordinary mortals.

At least, that is what Dungeons and Dragons, or other fantasy genres might have us believe. The reality has less romance and hyperbole. In their essence, a wizard is a scholar of life, the natural world, and our interaction with the universe. A wizard collects knowledge and experience to increase their wisdom and understanding. For magic is just another word for forces that we do not fully understand, and wizards explore the borders of what is known and what is unknown.

Wizardry: The Art of Shaping Reality: Wizardry is the embodiment of a profound understanding of the hidden workings of the universe. An intricate blend of knowledge, intuition, and wisdom allows the wizard to tap into the fundamental forces underpinning existence. Through rigorous study, intense training, and a deep connection with the mystical realms, a wizard may acquire the ability to understand these forces, adapting to the natural course of events and flowing with them towards desired outcomes.

Famous Wizards from History: Throughout the annals of human civilization, several figures have emerged as renowned wizards. From the mythical and legendary Merlin, advisor to King Arthur and renowned practitioner of the magical arts, to Paracelsus, the influential alchemist of the Renaissance, history is replete with individuals whose mastery of arcane knowledge shaped the world in profound ways. Each of these historical wizards left an indelible mark on their respective eras, demonstrating the immense power and potential that wizardry holds.

Paracelsus, born Philippus Aureolus Theophrastus Bombastus von Hohenheim, was an immensely influential figure in the world of alchemy during the Renaissance era. Born in Switzerland in the early 16th century, Paracelsus revolutionized the field of medicine by incorporating alchemical principles into his practice. He challenged the traditional medical knowledge of his time and emphasized the importance of observation and experimentation. Paracelsus believed in the concept of "like cures like" and advocated the use of specific herbal remedies and minerals to treat various ailments. His innovative approach to medicine and alchemy laid the foundation for modern pharmaceutical practices. Paracelsus's writings, such as his magnum opus "Theophrastus Bombastus von Hohenheim," continue to be studied and revered by scholars interested in the history of alchemy and medicine.

Famous Wizards in Fiction: The realm of fiction has also birthed a multitude of iconic wizard characters, captivating readers, and viewers alike. Gandalf, the wise and venerable wizard from J.R.R. Tolkien's Middle-earth, and Albus Dumbledore, the benevolent headmaster of Hogwarts School of Witchcraft and Wizardry in J.K. Rowling's Harry Potter series stand as paragons of wisdom and power. These fictional wizards, among many others, continue to inspire and ignite our imagination, showcasing the limitless possibilities of wizardry in the realm of storytelling.

The symbolism of the Magician Tarot Card: In the mystical world of tarot, the Magician card holds a significant place. Depicted as a figure standing at a table adorned with various tools and symbols, the Magician represents the embodiment of power, creativity, and manifestation. This card is often numbered as the first card of the Major Arcana, signifying the beginning of a transformative journey.

The Magician is depicted as a master of the elements, with one hand pointing toward the heavens and the other toward the earth. This gesture represents the connection between the spiritual and the physical realms, suggesting the Magician's ability to channel the divine. The table before the Magician is adorned with four elemental symbols: a cup, a sword, a pentacle, and a wand, representing the realms of emotions, intellect, materiality, and intuition, respectively.

The Magician card is closely associated with the planet Mercury, the Roman god of communication, intellect, and skill. This association further emphasizes the Magician's ability to harness the power of words, thoughts, and actions to manifest desires and bring about change. The infinity symbol above the Magician's head represents limitless potential and the infinite possibilities available to those who align themselves with their inner power.

The Magician card encourages the seeker to embrace their innate abilities and talents. It urges them to tap into their creative energies and use their skills to manifest their aspirations. It serves as a reminder that the power to shape one's reality lies within, and with focus, determination, and clear intent, anything is possible. Furthermore, the Magician card embodies the concept of transformation and personal growth. It suggests that the seeker has reached a point in their journey where they are ready to harness their inner power and utilize it to bring about positive transformations in their life. It signifies a time of self-discovery, where the seeker can explore their true potential and take confident steps forward.

The Magician card often indicates that the seeker has the necessary skills, resources, and opportunities to achieve their goals and desires. The card encourages them to take action and make use of their abilities to manifest their dreams into reality. It may also serve as a reminder for the seeker to be mindful of their thoughts, words, and actions, emphasizing the importance of clarity and focus in directing one's energy toward the desired outcome.

In some cases, the Magician card may suggest that the seeker is not fully aware of their own power and potential. It serves as a gentle nudge to explore their abilities, talents, and interests, and to recognize the influence they can have in their own life and the lives of others.

Overall, the appearance of the Magician card in a tarot reading signifies the presence of great potential, personal empowerment, and the ability to manifest one's desires through focused intention and action. It invites the seeker to embrace their inner power and take charge of their destiny, confident in their ability to create positive change.

Embarking on the Path of Wizardry: To become a wizard is to embark on an extraordinary journey of knowledge, discipline, and self-discovery. It requires a commitment to the pursuit of wisdom and the cultivation of a profound connection with the forces that permeate our world. As we venture deeper into the realms of wizardry, we shall explore the underlying principles, the secrets of spellcraft, and the profound responsibilities that accompany such power. Only by delving into the realms of magic and embracing the essence of wizardry can one truly be ready to participate in the broader community as a wizard.

Wizards can be found in many different backgrounds and cultures. As such, we should embrace diversity and inclusivity, recognizing that people of all races, genders, abilities, and identities can embody the qualities of a wizard. Wizards encourage and support others on their own paths to personal growth and mastery. A truly wise person recognizes the importance of empathy and compassion, treating others with kindness and respect, and trying to understand their perspectives and experiences. Use your knowledge and abilities to help and uplift others, contributing positively to the world around you. Remember, being a wizard is about embracing knowledge, wisdom, creativity, empathy, and self-discipline. Using these tools, you can embark on a journey of personal growth and become your own version of a modern-day wizard.

Chapter Two – Merlin the Arch-Druid

"Merlin is the wisest and most powerful magician of all time, his knowledge and abilities are unmatched." – Unknown

"In every age, there comes a time when a true magician is needed. That time is now, and that magician is Merlin." - Arthurian legend

"Merlin, the enigmatic sorcerer, weaver of destinies and guardian of the mystical realm, his name echoes through the ages, a testament to his enduring legacy." - Unknown

In the vast tapestry of Arthurian mythology, one enigmatic figure stands out amongst the rest - Merlin the Magician. Known for his wisdom, mystical powers, and instrumental role in the life of King Arthur, Merlin has captured the imaginations of countless generations. However, the true identity and origins of this legendary figure remain shrouded in mystery. Scholars and storytellers alike have put forth various theories to unravel the enigma of Merlin.

The first theory suggests that Merlin was a historical figure who lived during the late 5th and early 6th centuries. Some believe that he was a Welsh bard and advisor to several Welsh kings. According to this theory, the tales of Merlin's magical abilities and prophecies might have originated from the embellishment of his historical accomplishments over time.

Another theory proposes that Merlin was an amalgamation of multiple individuals, blending the stories and deeds of various wise men, druids, and seers from different periods. This notion supports the idea that Merlin could be a title rather than a singular name. In this interpretation, "Merlin" would represent a lineage or succession of magical advisors to the kings of Britain, each passing down their knowledge and power to the next in line.

Furthermore, some legends depict Merlin as the offspring of a mortal woman and an otherworldly being, such as a demon or an incubus. This lineage would grant him supernatural abilities and make him a bridge between the human and magical realms. This theory suggests that Merlin's incredible powers were inherited rather than learned.

Speaking of his powers, Merlin possessed a vast array of magical abilities, surpassing those of any other mortal. His foremost talent lay in his gift of foresight, which allowed him to glimpse into the future and make prophecies. He possessed unparalleled knowledge of the arcane arts, including the ability to shape-shift, manipulate the elements, and communicate with animals. It was said that Merlin could summon storms, heal the wounded, and create powerful illusions.

However, Merlin's powers were not limited to magic alone. He possessed great wisdom and intellect, which he employed to advise and guide Arthur during his rise to power. Merlin was instrumental in the conception and construction of Arthur's legendary sword, Excalibur, and the establishment of the Round Table. His counsel proved invaluable in Arthur's quests and battles, allowing the young king to make wise decisions and avoid disastrous pitfalls.

Merlin's greatest feat, perhaps, was his role in the defense of Britain against its enemies. His magical prowess played a crucial part in Arthur's victories, ensuring the unity and prosperity of the realm. In some tales, Merlin used his powers to manipulate the fates of individuals, subtly nudging events in the desired direction. Yet, he remained an elusive figure, often vanishing and reappearing at crucial moments, leaving behind only his enigmatic presence and echoes of his wisdom.

Ultimately, the true nature and identity of Merlin the Magician may forever elude us. Whether he was a historical advisor, a mythical figure, or a title passed down through generations, the tales of Merlin's exploits continue to captivate the hearts and minds of those who hear them. His legacy lives on as the epitome of magical prowess, wisdom, and the driving force behind the destiny of Britain and its fabled king, Arthur.

Merlin's wisdom and magical prowess are widely known. He was an advisor to various kings and played a crucial role in the rise of King Arthur. Merlin guided Arthur's father, Uther Pendragon, in his quest to seduce Igraine, the wife of Duke Gorlois of Cornwall. This union resulted in the birth of Arthur, who would later become the legendary King of Camelot. Throughout Arthur's reign, Merlin offered guidance, providing strategic advice, and using his magical abilities to aid the king and his knights.

Merlin had a mystical connection with the Lady of the Lake, a powerful enchantress associated with the magical island of Avalon. It was the Lady of the Lake who bestowed upon Arthur the legendary sword Excalibur. Merlin acted as a conduit between Arthur and the Lady, serving as a guardian and intermediary of sacred knowledge and spiritual energy. He understood the importance of balance and harmony between the mortal realm and the mystical realms, and through his connection with the Lady of the Lake, he facilitated this connection for Arthur.

In some versions of the Arthurian legend, Merlin's life takes a tragic turn when he falls in love with a young sorceress named Nimue, also known as the Lady of the Lake. Nimue became Merlin's apprentice, and her cunning and magical abilities surpassed even his own. Eventually, Nimue betrayed Merlin, trapping him in a cave or beneath a stone, sealing his powers and knowledge within. This event marked the end of Merlin's active involvement in the world of mortals, as he became a figure of myth and legend.

Merlin's life offers several lessons and serves as an archetype for wizardry. His wisdom, foresight, and magical abilities symbolize the power of knowledge and the importance of understanding the interconnectedness of the universe. Merlin's role as an advisor to kings emphasizes the importance of using wisdom and magic responsibly, for the greater good of society. His relationship with the stars and universal energy highlights the idea that everything is interconnected, and that understanding and harnessing this energy can bring about great change. The story of Merlin also teaches us about the dangers of pride and the limitations of power, as seen through his downfall at the hands of Nimue.

Ultimately, Merlin embodies the idea of the wise and powerful sorcerer, offering inspiration for those who seek knowledge, balance, and the responsible use of power.

Just as Merlin offered a valuable service to the kings of Britain, so too, can a modern-day wizard give their time to better their local community. A wizard could indeed set up a house, shop, or library in a town and help the community in unique and magical ways. The wizard would need to acquire a suitable location for their establishment, whether it's a house, shop, or spooky tower. This could involve purchasing or renting a property, depending on the circumstances. Once the wizard has secured the location, they can use their magical abilities to enchant the premises. This could involve casting spells of protection, enhancing the building's appearance, or creating enchanting displays. For a shop or library, the wizard would need to acquire a diverse collection of magical items, books, or scrolls that cater to the interests and needs of the local community. These items could include potions, enchanted artifacts, spell books, and other mystical tools. As a wizard, they would possess a wealth of knowledge and expertise in various magical fields. They can provide services such as magical consultations, divination, potion brewing, spellcasting, and even magical creature taming or training. These services could be tailored to the specific needs of the local community.

The wizard can act as a trusted advisor and guide for the local people. They can offer advice on matters of importance or problem-solving that involves thinking outside of the box. The wizard's wisdom and experience extend beyond the magical realm, providing guidance on personal matters, decision-making, and other areas of life. The wizard can organize and host magical events, workshops, and classes for the community. Such events would not only entertain and educate the locals but also foster a sense of community and camaraderie.

Overall, the presence of a wizard in the town would offer a unique blend of magical services, advice, and guidance to the local people. By sharing their magical expertise and using their mystical abilities, the wizard would not only serve the community but also enrich the lives of its inhabitants with the wonders and benefits of magic.

Chapter Three – Odin and the Magical Runes

"I know that I hung on a windy tree for nine long nights, wounded with a spear, dedicated to Odin, myself to myself, on that tree of which no man knows from where its roots run." - Odin, Hávamál

"Odin carved the runes with the knowledge of mighty songs." - Poetic Edda, Voluspa

"I know spells, no king's wife can say, and no man has mastered." - Odin, Hávamál

In the rich tapestry of Norse mythology, few figures stand as tall and enigmatic as the god Odin. Known as the Allfather, he is the chief deity of the Norse Pantheon and the ruler of Asgard. Odin possesses an array of magical powers that set him apart from other gods, and his mastery of runes and Norse magic is particularly noteworthy. Through his deep understanding of the cosmos and his unyielding quest for knowledge, Odin wields magic as a potent tool to shape the world around him.

Odin's insatiable thirst for knowledge and wisdom is exemplified in this quote from the ancient Norse poem, Hávamál. In his relentless pursuit of cosmic understanding, Odin sought to gain the secrets of the universe through personal sacrifice. He hung himself from the World Tree, Yggdrasil, for nine arduous nights, deprived of food and water, pierced by his own spear. Through this agonizing ordeal, Odin attuned himself to the magical forces that flow within the realms, allowing him to perceive and harness powerful runes and divine magic.

According to the Poetic Edda, Odin obtained the knowledge of runes by self-inflicting a wound upon himself with a spear and hanging on Yggdrasil, sacrificing himself to himself once more. This supreme act of self-sacrifice granted him the ability to perceive and shape the cosmic energies encapsulated within each rune. With his deep understanding of the runes, Odin acquired the power to alter fate, communicate with spirits, and channel magic that could affect the natural and supernatural realms.

As the Allfather, he boasts knowledge of spells that surpass even the most learned individuals in the Norse mythological world. These spells grant Odin the ability to bend reality, control the elements, and shape destinies. Moreover, his magic extends beyond the boundaries of the physical world, enabling him to traverse realms, communicate with spirits, and even foretell the future. This profound understanding of magic makes Odin an unparalleled force in the mythological pantheon.

Odin's Influence on Gandalf:

J.R.R. Tolkien, the renowned author of "The Lord of the Rings" trilogy, drew inspiration from various mythologies, legends, and folklore when creating his characters and stories. While Tolkien never explicitly stated that Odin directly influenced the character of Gandalf, there are several similarities between them that suggest a possible connection.

Odin, also known as Woden by the Anglo-Saxons, is a prominent figure in Norse mythology. Odin is associated with wisdom, magic, poetry, and prophecy. He is often depicted as an old man with a long white beard, wearing a wide-brimmed hat and a cloak, and carrying a staff or spear.

Gandalf, also known as Mithrandir or Greyhame, is one of the central characters in Tolkien's Middle-earth legendarium. He is a wizard and a member of the Istari, a group of powerful beings sent to Middle Earth to help in the struggle against the dark forces. Gandalf is portrayed as an old man with a long white beard, wearing a wide-brimmed hat and a grey cloak. He wields a staff and possesses great wisdom, magical abilities, and foresight.

Both are wise, mysterious, and powerful figures who guide and assist mortals in their quests. They share physical attributes such as the long white beard and the distinctive hat and cloak. Both Odin and Gandalf are associated with magic, wisdom, and prophecy, and they play pivotal roles in their respective mythologies.

It is worth noting that Tolkien was a scholar of mythology, and he drew inspiration from a wide range of sources, including Norse, Celtic, and Germanic mythologies. While it is not confirmed that Odin directly inspired Gandalf, it is likely that Tolkien's knowledge of Norse mythology and his fascination with its rich characters and themes influenced the development of his wizard character. Tolkien's deep knowledge of mythology and his ability to weave elements from different traditions into his own mythos contributed to the richness and depth of his characters, including Gandalf.

Odin's magical powers in Norse mythology are a testament to his unwavering dedication to knowledge and his willingness to undergo extreme sacrifices. Through his mastery of runes and his ability to tap into the mystical forces of the cosmos, Odin weaves the magic that shapes the fate of gods and mortals alike. From his self-imposed ordeals to his deep connection with the runes, Odin's magical abilities epitomize the blending of wisdom, sacrifice, and supernatural power. As the Allfather, he stands as the ultimate embodiment of the mystical and magical aspects of Norse mythology, forever inspiring awe, and fascination among those who delve into the enchanting world of Norse lore.

Odin's Quest for Knowledge and the Runes

Few figures stand as prominently as Odin in Norse Mythology, the Allfather and king of the Aesir gods. Among his many attributes, Odin is renowned for his insatiable thirst for knowledge and personal quest to acquire the wisdom of the runes. During this journey, Odin undertook many trials in pursuit of this sacred knowledge.

The runes, ancient symbols with magical properties, held immense power in the Norse realm. They were not merely a form of writing but also encapsulated deep wisdom and divine insight. Odin, ever the seeker of knowledge, desired to unravel their secrets and harness their might. However, the path to obtaining this knowledge was fraught with challenges.

Odin knew that the runes were guarded by the primordial well of Urd, located beneath the roots of the world tree, Yggdrasil. To gain access to this well, Odin realized that he had to undergo a transformative journey, one that mirrored the arduous process of learning.

Firstly, Odin sacrificed himself to himself. He hung himself from the branches of Yggdrasil for nine nights, pierced by his own spear. This symbolic act represented the sacrifice required to obtain true wisdom. In this self-imposed ordeal, Odin deprived himself of the physical senses, entering a state of profound introspection. Similarly, when approaching knowledge, individuals must commit themselves to the process, dedicating time, and effort, often sacrificing other activities to acquire new skills.

During his self-sacrifice, Odin suffered hunger and thirst, endured the elements, and confronted his deepest fears. These trials tested his resolve and determination. In the same way, individuals often face challenges, whether it be overcoming difficulties in comprehension, deciphering complex ideas, or battling self-doubt. Like Odin, they must persevere and confront their limitations to progress in their journey toward knowledge.

As Odin approached the brink of death, the runes finally revealed themselves to him. From the depths of his self-imposed suffering, he plucked the sacred knowledge he sought. This profound revelation, the culmination of his quest, filled Odin with immense wisdom and power. He emerged as the master of the runes, wielding their magic with unmatched prowess.

The parallels between Odin's quest for the runes and the magical journey are striking. Just as Odin embarked on a transformative quest, learners undertake their own odyssey toward learning. They start from a place of ignorance, gradually acquiring the fundamentals of knowledge, then gaining a deeper understanding.

The process of learning involves trial and error, perseverance, and self-reflection. Learners face countless obstacles, be it deciphering complex information or developing critical thinking skills. Like Odin's sacrifice, the path to knowledge demands discipline, dedication, and an unwavering commitment to personal growth.

Odin's quest for knowledge and the runes exemplifies the transformative nature of learning. The trials he undertook mirror the challenges faced by individuals seeking to acquire new skills in the modern world. Just as Odin emerged as the master of the runes, learners who persevere and embrace the journey unlock a world of possibilities and empowerment. The pursuit of knowledge, whether in the realm of ancient mythology or contemporary education, remains a transformative and empowering endeavor.

Chapter Four – Gender-Diverse Wizards

Throughout history, remarkable women have emerged as powerful practitioners of magic, revered for their extraordinary abilities and profound impact on their respective cultures. Similarly, some figures from myths and legends have been quite fluid in their genders, swapping from one to another, or remaining asexual. From ancient civilizations to modern times, these legendary figures have captivated the imaginations of countless generations. In the following chapters, we will explore the lives and powers of some of the most famous wizards, sorcerers, and magicians from diverse backgrounds and cultures across the globe.

Circe the Enchanter:
First, let's look at Circe, a powerful figure from Greek Mythology. Circe, the enchantress, possessed an unparalleled command over potions and spells. With her knowledge of herbs and incantations, she transformed her enemies into animals and deceived Odysseus' crew during their journey home from the Trojan War. Circe's abilities extended beyond manipulation, making her a potent sorceress feared by mortals and gods alike.

Circe was the daughter of the sun god Helios and the Oceanid nymph Perse. She had siblings, including Aeetes, the king of Colchis, and Pasiphae, the mother of the Minotaur. Despite being a lesser-known goddess, Circe possessed great magical abilities and was considered a formidable force.

She was a powerful enchanter and sorcerer who played a significant role in the adventures of Odysseus, the hero of the poem. Circe possessed the ability to use magic and transform humans into animals. She was skilled in the art of potions and spells, often using them to manipulate and control others. Her most famous ability was the power of transformation, which allowed her to turn men into animals, particularly swine.

This transformation symbolizes an esoteric journey, highlighting the distinction between the human and animal nature. By transforming the men into swine, Circe exposed their base and instinctual tendencies. The men, reduced to the form of beasts, represent the loss of human rationality and self-control. It is only through Odysseus' resilience and the intervention of the god Hermes that he avoids the same fate, ultimately freeing his crew from Circe's enchantment.

Circe has been interpreted in various ways by scholars and writers throughout history. Some consider her a symbol of temptation and danger, representing the allure of sensual pleasure that can lead men astray from their quests. Others view her as a symbol of transformation and personal growth, as Odysseus learns valuable lessons during his time with her.

Circe's myths offer several lessons and teachings. They caution against succumbing to temptation and falling into destructive behaviors. Circe's transformation of Odysseus' men into swine serves as a warning about the consequences of indulging in excessive desires. Additionally, Circe's character emphasizes the importance of wisdom and guidance in one's journey. Odysseus learns valuable information and receives guidance from Circe, helping him navigate the challenges he faces on his quest. This highlights the significance of seeking advice, learning from others, and making wise choices.

Overall, Circe's myths present a complex figure who represents both danger and wisdom. Her stories provide valuable insights into human nature, the temptations we face, and the potential for personal growth and transformation.

Loki the Trickster:

Loki, a trickster god in Norse mythology, is known for his shapeshifting abilities. He is portrayed as both male and female at different times, occasionally taking on feminine forms. In one tale, Loki transforms into a mare and becomes impregnated by a stallion, resulting in the birth of the eight-legged horse Sleipnir. Loki's gender fluidity reflects the fluid nature of his character and serves to blur boundaries and challenge societal expectations.

Coyote:

In Native American folklore, Coyote is a prominent trickster figure found in various tribes' mythology. Coyote often embodies both masculine and feminine qualities, blurring the lines between genders. In some stories, Coyote is depicted as changing genders or taking on dual gender identities. These tales emphasize the fluidity and interconnectedness of gender and reflect the cultural acceptance of diverse gender expressions within indigenous communities.

Two-Spirit:

While not specific to a single individual, the concept of "Two-Spirit" exists among several indigenous cultures in North America. Two-Spirit refers to individuals who embody both masculine and feminine qualities and often possess spiritual or shamanic abilities. They are seen as having a unique perspective and are often revered within their communities. Two-Spirit people challenge the Western gender binary and serve as a reminder of the diversity and fluidity of gender expression.

What we can learn from these stories and characters is the importance of embracing and respecting gender diversity. These myths challenge rigid gender norms and show that gender can be fluid and exist beyond a binary framework. They remind us to acknowledge and honor individuals who don't fit traditional gender categories, fostering a more inclusive and accepting society. Additionally, these tales highlight the significance of self-expression and self-acceptance, allowing individuals to embrace their authentic identities, regardless of societal expectations.

Isis:

Isis is an Egyptian goddess associated with various attributes such as motherhood, magic, healing, fertility, and the throne. She is considered the wife and sister of Osiris, the god of the afterlife, and the mother of Horus, the falcon-headed god associated with kingship. Isis was worshipped as a powerful deity and often depicted with wings outstretched, representing her protective nature.

In terms of magic, Isis is known for her mastery of magical arts. She is often portrayed as a skilled magician and an adept healer. According to Egyptian mythology, Isis used her magical abilities to heal her husband Osiris after he was killed by their brother Seth. She also used her magical prowess to protect and assist her son Horus in his battle against Seth.

What we can learn from Isis is the power of magic as a transformative and healing force. Her teachings emphasize the importance of using magic for positive purposes, such as healing, protection, and nurturing. Isis also embodies the concept of feminine power, showcasing the strength, resilience, and wisdom associated with the divine feminine.

Ishtar:

Ishtar is an ancient Mesopotamian goddess, primarily worshipped in the Babylonian and Assyrian civilizations. She is the goddess of love, beauty, fertility, war, and sex. Ishtar is often associated with the planet Venus and is considered a powerful and passionate deity.

In relation to magic, Ishtar's association with love and sexuality suggests a connection to the transformative and creative aspects of magic. Love spells, fertility rituals, and rituals aimed at invoking desire are often attributed to Ishtar. As a goddess of war, she also symbolizes the power to protect and fight for one's desires and rights.

Ishtar's teachings emphasize embracing one's desires and passions while recognizing the transformative potential of these energies. She reminds us of the importance of balance and understanding in navigating our own desires, relationships, and the world around us. Ishtar also teaches us to harness our inner strength and courage to stand up for ourselves and what we believe in.

Freyja:

Freyja is a Norse goddess associated with love, beauty, and fertility. She is a member of the Vanir, one of the two main groups of deities in Norse mythology. Freyja is often depicted as a powerful and sensual goddess, with a love for jewelry, beauty, and sensuality. Freyja teaches us to embrace our sensuality and celebrate our own beauty and desires. As a goddess of love, Freyja emphasizes the importance of nurturing and cherishing our relationships with others. Freyja's association with fertility reminds us of the cycles of nature and the importance of respecting and honoring the natural world.

Hecate:

Hecate is an ancient Greek goddess associated with magic, witchcraft, and crossroads. She is often depicted as a triple-faced goddess, representing her ability to see into the past, present, and future. Hecate is also associated with night, the moon, and the underworld. Hecate teaches us to embrace our own personal power, particularly in the realm of magic and intuition. She encourages us to trust our instincts and tap into our inner wisdom. Hecate's association with the underworld and crossroads reminds us of the importance of embracing the unknown and navigating through life's uncertainties with courage and clarity. Hecate symbolizes the darkness and the shadow aspects of our psyche. By acknowledging and integrating our shadow self, we can achieve greater wholeness and self-awareness.

Brigid:

Brigid is a Celtic goddess associated with healing, poetry, smithcraft, and fertility. She is revered as a triple goddess, embodying the aspects of maiden, mother, and crone. Brigid is also associated with fire, creativity, and inspiration. Brigid inspires us to tap into our creative potential and express ourselves through various forms of art, poetry, and craftsmanship. As a goddess of healing, Brigid reminds us of the importance of nurturing our physical, emotional, and spiritual well-being. She offers guidance and support in times of transformation and rebirth. Brigid is also associated with community and hospitality. She encourages us to foster a sense of belonging, support one another, and create a harmonious and inclusive environment.

These deities offer rich symbolism and teachings that can inspire and guide us in various aspects of our lives, including self-expression, relationships, personal power, healing, creativity, connection to nature, and wisdom. As wizards, we do not have to necessarily worship them or even think of them as real entities. Wizards come from all walks of life and from many different spiritual or philosophical backgrounds. But the stories of these mythological figures may offer lessons for us to share.

Chapter Five – Baba Yaga the Guardian of Mysteries

In the deep recesses of Slavic folklore, amidst the shadowy realms of myth and magic, resides a figure both feared and revered—a haggard crone known as Baba Yaga. Her name echoes through the ages, conjuring images of dark forests, dancing birch trees, and enchanted cottages on chicken legs. Baba Yaga, a powerful and enigmatic character, is a staple in the tales and legends of Eastern Europe.

Legend has it that Baba Yaga's origins are as mysterious as the depths of the forests she calls home. Some say she is a witch, while others believe she is a nature spirit or a goddess of the wilderness. Regardless of her true nature, Baba Yaga's stories are woven with supernatural feats and strange encounters.

Among the tales associated with Baba Yaga, one of the most famous revolves around her abode—an unusual hut perched upon a single chicken leg. This whimsical dwelling is said to wander through the forest, following no predictable path. To enter the hut, one must utter the words, "Little hut, little hut, turn your back to the forest and your front to me." Those who are pure-hearted and kind-hearted are granted entry, while those who are wicked or impure are met with peril.

Baba Yaga herself is a figure of immense power. She is said to possess vast knowledge of herbs, spells, and ancient rituals. She can control the elements, summon storms, and transform herself into various creatures at will. Baba Yaga's powers are both fearsome and awe-inspiring, making her a force to be reckoned with.

The old crone's dwelling place reflects her enigmatic nature. Deep within the heart of the forest, hidden from prying eyes, lies Baba Yaga's hut—an embodiment of magic and mystery. The surrounding woods are shrouded in an air of otherworldly enchantment, with whispering trees and glowing mushrooms illuminating the path for those brave enough to seek her wisdom.

Despite her fearsome reputation, Baba Yaga is known to be a complex character. She is neither wholly good nor wholly evil, but rather a guardian of the natural order. Baba Yaga represents the untamed forces of nature and the wild aspects of the human psyche. She imparts valuable lessons to those who dare to venture into her domain through her tales.

One of the lessons Baba Yaga teaches is the importance of self-reliance and resourcefulness. Many who seek her help are tasked with seemingly impossible challenges, such as retrieving a rare magical item or completing a treacherous quest. Baba Yaga encourages individuals to tap into their inner strength and intelligence, showing them they possess the necessary tools to overcome obstacles.

Another lesson Baba Yaga imparts is the need for balance and respect in our relationship with nature. She reminds us that the natural world is not ours to conquer, but rather a realm to be revered and protected. Baba Yaga's deep connection to the wilderness serves as a reminder of the interconnectedness of all living things and the importance of preserving the delicate balance of the Earth.

Ultimately, Baba Yaga stands as a powerful symbol of the enigmatic and mystical aspects of life. Her stories remind us that the world is filled with wonders yet to be discovered and that the path to wisdom often lies in the unexplored territories of our hearts and minds. Through her trials and tests, Baba Yaga offers us the opportunity to embrace our own power, confront our fears, and unlock the hidden magic within ourselves.

Nature is a remarkable teacher, offering an abundance of wisdom for those willing to observe and learn. From the grandeur of mountains to the tranquility of a babbling brook, nature provides us with countless opportunities to reconnect with ourselves and the world around us. Beyond its aesthetic appeal, spending time in nature has been recognized as a powerful means to enhance our mental and physical well-being.

In the midst of our fast-paced and often stressful lives, immersing ourselves in nature can be a much-needed respite. The serene beauty and quietude of natural environments create a soothing atmosphere that helps to calm the mind and reduce stress levels. The sights, sounds, and scents of nature have a way of grounding us, allowing us to escape the noise and distractions of modern life. Whether it's a walk through a forest, a hike in the mountains, or a stroll along the beach, these experiences provide a sense of peace and tranquility that can be immensely beneficial for our mental health.

Moreover, spending time outside in nature allows us to engage in physical activities that are both enjoyable and beneficial for our bodies. Nature offers a vast playground for outdoor recreation, inviting us to explore, hike, swim, bike, or simply take a leisurely stroll. These activities promote physical fitness and encourage us to be more active and lead a healthier lifestyle. Being in nature inspires movement and fosters a sense of adventure, which can make exercise feel more like a joyful pursuit rather than a chore.

Another significant benefit of spending time in nature is the exposure to sunlight. Sunlight is a vital source of vitamin D, a nutrient crucial for our physical well-being. By spending time outdoors, we allow our bodies to soak up the sun's rays and naturally synthesize this essential vitamin. Vitamin D plays a vital role in bone health, immune function, and mental well-being. It is known to boost mood, alleviate symptoms of depression, and regulate sleep patterns. By enjoying the outdoors, we not only nourish our bodies with the sunlight they need but also reap the associated health benefits.

Beyond the mental and physical benefits, nature has a way of humbling us and instilling a sense of interconnectedness. Observing the intricate patterns of a flower, the grace of a soaring bird, or the resilience of a mighty tree reminds us of the wisdom and harmony inherent in the natural world. Nature teaches us patience, adaptability, and resilience as we witness the cycles of growth, change, and renewal.

In a world driven by technology and constant connectivity, it is crucial to make time to disconnect and reconnect with the natural world. Whether it's a brief walk in a nearby park or a more immersive wilderness experience, spending time in nature offers a wealth of wisdom and benefits for our overall well-being. It provides solace for our minds, invigoration for our bodies, and a profound sense of connection to something larger than ourselves. Let us cherish and protect the natural spaces that have so much to teach us, for in them, we find both solace and inspiration.

Chapter Six – Amara the Wise

African folklore is a treasure trove of captivating tales and mythical characters. Among them, Amara stands as a revered sorcerer, whose stories have been passed down through generations. This chapter delves into a fascinating story surrounding Amara, exploring her magical powers, remarkable adventures, and the timeless wisdom hidden within her stories. For the purposes of cultural sensitivity, several ideas have been amalgamated in the form of a fictional character based on many African legends about wise women.

Amara, also known as the Enchanter of Wisdom, hailed from a remote village nestled deep within the heart of West Africa. Born under a dazzling moonlit night, she possessed an otherworldly aura from an early age. As her powers grew, so did her reputation, spreading far and wide across the lands.

One of the most renowned stories associated with Amara revolves around her encounter with the talking trees. Legend has it that deep within a mystical forest, a grove of ancient trees possessed the ability to communicate with those who sought wisdom. Many ventured into the forest, but none returned with the wisdom they sought. Determined to uncover their secrets, Amara embarked on a perilous journey. Through her profound understanding of nature and unwavering perseverance, she successfully conversed with the talking trees. The lessons she learned from these wise guardians of the forest became a source of inspiration for seekers of wisdom throughout the ages.

This tale teaches us the importance of patience, perseverance, and respect for nature. Amara's success was not instant; it required both dedication and a deep connection with the natural world. The story reminds us that wisdom is not easily obtained, but with tenacity and respect, it can be discovered even in the most unexpected places.

In another captivating legend, Amara's prowess as a sorcerer is put to the test during a dance competition. A neighboring kingdom held a grand celebration, where dancers from across the land gathered to compete. Recognizing Amara's extraordinary abilities, the king invited her to participate. She accepted the challenge, but little did she know that her fellow competitors were skilled in dark magic. As each dancer showcased their enchantments, Amara relied on her innate wisdom, employing her powers of light and grace. With every move, she outshone her rivals, mesmerizing the audience and revealing the true essence of her enchantment.

The story of the Dance of Shadows emphasizes the importance of staying true to oneself. Amara faced adversity and temptation but remained steadfast in her commitment to her own unique talents. In a world often driven by competition and comparison, this tale reminds us that true power and beauty lie in embracing our individual gifts and expressing them authentically.

One of the most profound tales linked to Amara revolves around her pursuit of balance between the physical and spiritual realms. Guided by her inner wisdom, she embarked on a solitary quest, seeking equilibrium in a world plagued by disharmony. Her journey took her to sacred sites and mystical realms, where she encountered powerful spirits and entities. Through her interactions and the challenges she faced, Amara unravelled the secrets of balance, ultimately becoming a beacon of harmony herself.

The Quest for Balance teaches us the importance of seeking equilibrium in our lives. It emphasizes the interconnectedness of the physical and spiritual realms and encourages us to nurture both aspects of our existence. Amara's journey inspires us to explore our own paths toward balance and to recognize that true harmony can only be achieved through introspection, understanding, and respect for the interconnectedness of all things.

Amara continues to captivate the hearts and minds of those who delve into African folklore. Her stories embody timeless lessons of patience, perseverance, authenticity, and balance. Through her remarkable adventures and extraordinary powers, Amara serves as a guiding light, reminding us of the importance of seeking wisdom and embracing our unique selves. In the annals of African folklore, Amara's legacy endures, inspiring generations to come with her magical tales of enlightenment and enchantment.

Amara possessed an extensive knowledge of herbs, rituals, and divination. She was often sought out for her ability to heal the sick, protect communities from malevolent spirits, and provide guidance in times of need. Amara's powers were deeply intertwined with African spiritual traditions and the wisdom of her ancestors.

Belief in magic is deeply rooted in the cultural and spiritual traditions of many African countries. While it is important to note that Africa is a diverse continent with a multitude of cultures and beliefs, there are several countries where belief in magic continues to be prevalent. It's worth mentioning that the perception and understanding of magic can vary across different regions and communities within these countries.

One such country is Nigeria, where a significant portion of the population adheres to traditional religious practices, including the belief in magic. Nigerian traditional religions, such as Yoruba, Igbo, and Hausa, incorporate magical beliefs and practices into their rituals. These practices often involve invoking spirits, using talismans, and engaging in divination to communicate with the spiritual realm.

Another country where belief in magic is widespread is South Africa. Traditional African beliefs, as well as the influence of various cultures and indigenous spiritual practices, contribute to the belief in magic. South African traditional healers, known as sangomas, play a significant role in magical practices. They are revered as intermediaries between the spiritual and physical worlds and are believed to possess supernatural powers and knowledge.

In other countries like Ghana, Kenya, and Tanzania, belief in magic is also present, although the specific practices and traditions may vary. These countries have diverse cultural backgrounds and indigenous beliefs that incorporate magical elements. The use of charms, amulets, and spells for protection, healing, and fortune is often part of the magical practices in these regions.

Witch doctors are a common trope in stories about African magicians that have made their way into European and American awareness. They should be more appropriately known as traditional healers and are important figures in many African societies. They are individuals who are believed to possess supernatural abilities and knowledge to heal physical and spiritual ailments. Traditional healers often use various methods, including herbal remedies, divination, and rituals, to diagnose and treat illnesses. They are consulted for a wide range of issues, including healing, protection, fertility, and guidance. Witch doctors are respected members of their communities and play a vital role in maintaining cultural traditions and spiritual practices.

It's important to approach the topic of belief in magic in African countries with cultural sensitivity and respect. These beliefs and practices are deeply ingrained in the cultural fabric of these societies and hold great significance for the people who adhere to them. Understanding and appreciating these diverse cultural traditions can provide valuable insights into the rich and varied heritage of African countries.

Chapter Seven – Chinese Alchemy and Mysticism

In the realms of wizards and alchemy, Chinese lore and legends unveil a treasure trove of mystical knowledge and profound wisdom. Over the centuries, Chinese culture has embraced the esoteric arts of alchemy and philosophy, weaving together practical experimentation, spiritual enlightenment, and a deep understanding of the natural world. As a student of magic, let's explore the lives, accomplishments, and enduring lessons of some of the most prominent historical alchemists and wizards from China.

Ge Hong (283-343 CE) is a revered figure in Chinese alchemy, Ge Hong was a polymath, philosopher, and adept alchemist. He authored the influential text "Baopuzi" (Master Who Embraces Simplicity), which compiled his extensive knowledge on various subjects, including Taoism, magic, immortality, and herbal medicine. Ge Hong developed techniques for the creation of elixirs and explored the concept of "inner alchemy," a spiritual practice focused on inner transformation and achieving immortality. His work emphasized the harmony between nature and humanity, encouraging individuals to cultivate virtue and live in harmony with the Dao.

Chinese inner alchemy, also known as Neidan or Nei Gong, is a spiritual and philosophical tradition that originated in ancient China. It is a form of internal cultivation aimed at transforming and refining one's inner self to achieve spiritual enlightenment and longevity. The practice of inner alchemy is deeply rooted in Taoist philosophy and draws upon principles such as the balance of Yin and Yang, the circulation of vital energy (Qi), and the attainment of immortality.

The main objective of Chinese inner alchemy is to harmonize and refine the three treasures of human existence: Jing (essence), Qi (vital energy), and Shen (spirit). It involves various practices, including meditation, breath control, visualization, movement exercises, dietary adjustments, and herbal medicine. The ultimate goal is to transmute the base substances of Jing and Qi into a more refined and spiritual form, thereby nourishing the Shen and achieving a higher state of consciousness.

Inner alchemy aims to cultivate the practitioner's spiritual and physical well-being, leading to increased vitality, enhanced health, mental clarity, emotional stability, and a deeper connection with the divine. It is believed that through the process of inner alchemy, one can attain immortality or spiritual liberation by transcending the limitations of the physical body.

To practice inner alchemy, individuals typically seek guidance from experienced teachers or masters who have studied and mastered the techniques and principles of this tradition. Practice requires discipline, patience, and dedication as it involves consistent training and self-cultivation over an extended period.

Ge Hong's teachings remind us of the importance of balance, both within ourselves and with the world around us. By nurturing our inner virtues and aligning our actions with the natural order, we can attain profound spiritual growth and find our path to enlightenment.

Some key aspects of inner alchemy practice:
- Meditation and Mindfulness: Cultivating stillness and focusing the mind to achieve a state of deep relaxation, tranquility, and inner peace.
- Breath Control: Regulating the breath to harmonize the flow of Qi in the body and cultivate a balanced energy system.
- Visualization: Using imagery and mental focus to guide and direct the flow of energy within the body, as well as to connect with higher realms of consciousness.
- Movement and Internal Exercises: Practicing specific physical movements, such as Tai Chi or Qi Gong, to cultivate and circulate Qi throughout the body, harmonizing its flow and promoting health and vitality.
- Diet and Herbal Medicine: Paying attention to the quality and balance of food intake, as well as incorporating herbal remedies that support energy cultivation and overall well-being.

It's important to note that Chinese inner alchemy is a profound and complex practice that requires guidance and dedicated study. It is deeply intertwined with Taoist philosophy and spirituality. While some aspects of inner alchemy can be adapted for general health and well-being, a comprehensive understanding and commitment to its principles are necessary to fully explore its transformative potential.

Wei Boyang (c. 2nd century CE): Wei Boyang, considered the father of Chinese alchemy, authored the "Zhouyi Cantong Qi" (The Kinship of the Three) - a seminal text that formed the foundation of Chinese alchemical practices. Wei Boyang believed that all matter was composed of two fundamental forces, the Yin and Yang, and sought to understand their interplay and transformation. His alchemical pursuits involved experiments with minerals, metals, and medicinal substances, aiming to transmute base elements into pure substances and unlock the secrets of immortality.

Wei Boyang teaches us the power of observation and experimentation in the pursuit of knowledge. By exploring the mysteries of nature and understanding its underlying principles, we can uncover profound truths and transform our perception of the world.

Sun Simiao (581-682 CE): Renowned as the "King of Medicine" in Chinese history, Sun Simiao was not only a skilled physician but also an accomplished alchemist and wizard. His seminal work, the "Qianjin Yaofang" (Essential Prescriptions Worth a Thousand Gold), served as a comprehensive guide to medicine, incorporating elements of alchemy and magic. Sun Simiao's writings emphasized the holistic approach to healthcare, advocating for the integration of physical, mental, and spiritual well-being. He believed that true healing extended beyond the treatment of symptoms, encompassing the nourishment of the soul and the cultivation of virtuous living.

Sun Simiao teaches us the importance of treating the root causes of our ailments, both in the physical and spiritual realms. By embracing a holistic approach to well-being and nurturing our inner virtues, we can achieve true health and harmony within ourselves.

These esteemed alchemists and wizards from Chinese lore have left an indelible mark on the world of esoteric knowledge. Their accomplishments, philosophies, and lessons continue to inspire seekers of wisdom and illuminate the path to enlightenment. By blending practical experimentation, spiritual introspection, and an unwavering connection with nature, they beckon us to embark on a transformative journey, unearthing the magic and wisdom that resides within our own souls.

Chapter Eight – Indian Wizards and Yogis

Indian culture has a rich and diverse tradition of magic users, wizards, and yogis, each with their unique practices and teachings. Let's explore these fascinating figures from history and legend and the lessons we can learn from them.

In Indian mythology and folklore, there are several legendary figures known for their magical abilities. One prominent example is Krishna, a central figure in the Hindu epic, the Mahabharata. Krishna possessed extraordinary powers and displayed his magic through various miraculous feats, such as lifting mountains, creating illusions, and performing divine acts.

Another notable figure is Ravana, the antagonist of the Hindu epic Ramayana. Ravana was a powerful sorcerer and the king of Lanka. He was known for his proficiency in dark arts and his ability to shape-shift, control celestial beings, and cast powerful spells.

Magic users in Indian culture often embody the idea that power should be used responsibly. Their stories remind us of the importance of self-control and using one's abilities for the greater good rather than personal gain.

In Indian folklore and literature, wizards are often depicted as knowledgeable and wise individuals who possess supernatural powers. One famous wizard is Bhirgu Muni, an ancient sage renowned for his expertise in astrology and the ability to predict future events accurately.

Another notable figure is Chanakya, also known as Kautilya or Vishnugupta. He was an ancient Indian scholar, economist, and strategist who served as the advisor to Emperor Chandragupta Maurya. Chanakya was known for his intellect, political acumen, and understanding of magical rituals to protect and enhance the kingdom.

Wizards in Indian culture teach us the importance of wisdom, knowledge, and foresight. They remind us to cultivate our intellect and use it for the betterment of society. They also emphasize the idea that power should be wielded with a sense of responsibility and integrity.

Yoga, an ancient Indian practice, involves physical, mental, and spiritual disciplines to attain self-realization and union with the divine. Yogis are individuals who have achieved an elevated level of mastery over their minds and bodies through dedicated practice.

One of the most famous yogis in history is Patanjali, who is credited with compiling the Yoga Sutras. These texts provide a systematic and philosophical framework for practicing and understanding yoga. Patanjali emphasized the eight limbs of yoga, which include ethical principles, physical postures, breath control, meditation, and concentration.

Yogis teach us the importance of self-discipline, self-awareness, and spiritual growth. They remind us of the transformative power of regular practice and the ability to achieve inner peace and harmony. Yogis also highlight the significance of maintaining balance in all aspects of life and cultivating a deeper connection with oneself and the world around us.

Overall, Indian magic users, wizards, and yogis offer valuable lessons about responsible use of power, wisdom, knowledge, self-discipline, and spiritual growth. Their stories and teachings continue to inspire individuals on the path of personal and spiritual development.

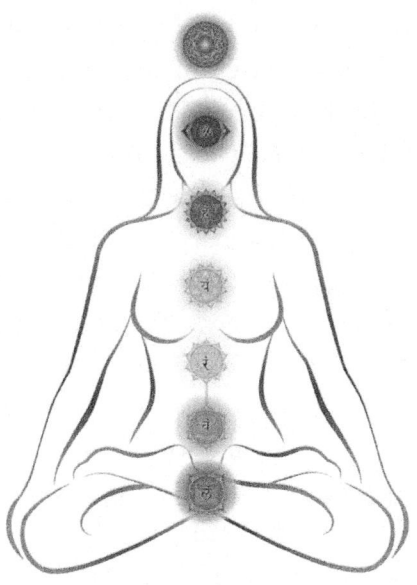

In Indian yoga philosophy, the seven chakras are considered as energy centers within the human body. These chakras are believed to be interconnected and aligned along the central channel, known as the "sushumna," which runs from the base of the spine to the crown of the head. Each chakra is associated with specific physical, emotional, and spiritual aspects of our being. By understanding and working with these chakras, one can strive for balance, well-being, and spiritual growth. Let's explore each of the seven chakras in detail:

Root Chakra (Muladhara): Located at the base of the spine, the root chakra is associated with stability, grounding, and a sense of security. It is symbolized by a red lotus with four petals. To meditate on the root chakra, sit in a comfortable position, close your eyes, and focus on the area at the base of your spine. Visualize a vibrant red energy spinning in a clockwise direction. Breathe deeply and affirm statements related to security, stability, and a sense of belonging.

To build the power of the root chakra, you can practice grounding activities such as walking barefoot on the earth, connecting with nature, or performing yoga poses that emphasize stability, such as the mountain pose (Tadasana).

Sacral Chakra (Svadhishthana): Located just below the navel, the sacral chakra is associated with creativity, sensuality, and emotional well-being. It is symbolized by an orange lotus with six petals. To meditate on the sacral chakra, sit comfortably, close your eyes, and focus on the area a few inches below the navel. Visualize a warm, orange energy swirling in a clockwise direction. Breathe deeply and affirm statements related to creativity, emotional expression, and pleasure.

To build the power of the sacral chakra, you can engage in activities that stimulate your creativity, such as painting, dancing, or writing. Engaging in sensual experiences, such as taking a relaxing bath or practicing self-care, can also support the flow of energy in this chakra.

Solar Plexus Chakra (Manipura): Located in the upper abdomen, the solar plexus chakra is associated with personal power, confidence, and self-esteem. It is symbolized by a yellow lotus with ten petals. To meditate on the solar plexus chakra, sit comfortably, close your eyes, and focus on the area between the navel and the sternum. Visualize a radiant yellow energy rotating in a clockwise direction. Breathe deeply and affirm statements related to personal power, self-worth, and confidence.

To build the power of the solar plexus chakra, you can practice activities that enhance your self-esteem and personal growth. This can include setting and achieving goals, engaging in positive affirmations, or practicing martial arts and other activities that promote self-discipline.

Heart Chakra (Anahata): Located at the center of the chest, the heart chakra is associated with love, compassion, and emotional balance. It is symbolized by a green lotus with twelve petals. To meditate on the heart chakra, sit comfortably, close your eyes, and focus on the area in the center of your chest. Visualize a beautiful, emerald green energy spinning in a clockwise direction. Breathe deeply and affirm statements related to love, compassion, and emotional healing.

To build the power of the heart chakra, you can engage in acts of kindness and cultivate compassion towards yourself and others. Practicing gratitude and forgiveness can also help open and balance this chakra.

Throat Chakra (Vishuddha): Located at the throat region, the throat chakra is associated with self-expression, communication, and authenticity. It is symbolized by a blue lotus with sixteen petals. To meditate on the throat chakra, sit comfortably, close your eyes, and focus on the area at the base of your throat. Visualize a vibrant blue energy rotating in a clockwise direction. Breathe deeply and affirm statements related to clear communication, self-expression, and speaking your truth.

To build the power of the throat chakra, you can engage in activities that encourage self-expression, such as singing, journaling, or engaging in honest and open communication. Practicing active listening and finding your authentic voice can also help balance this chakra.

Third Eye Chakra (Ajna): Located in the center of the forehead, between the eyebrows, the third eye chakra is associated with intuition, insight, and spiritual awareness. It is symbolized by an indigo lotus with two petals. To meditate on the third eye chakra, sit comfortably, close your eyes, and focus your attention on the space between your eyebrows. Visualize a deep indigo energy spinning in a clockwise direction. Breathe deeply and affirm statements related to intuition, wisdom, and inner knowing.

To build the power of the third eye chakra, you can engage in activities that stimulate your intuition, such as meditation, mindfulness, and dreamwork. Trusting your instincts and seeking inner guidance can also strengthen this chakra.

Crown Chakra (Sahasrara): Located at the top of the head, the crown chakra represents spiritual connection, higher consciousness, and transcendence. It is symbolized by a violet or white lotus with a thousand petals. To meditate on the crown chakra, sit comfortably, close your eyes, and visualize a radiant white or violet light at the top of your head. Breathe deeply and affirm statements related to spiritual connection, unity, and divine wisdom.

To build the power of the crown chakra, you can engage in practices that facilitate spiritual growth, such as meditation, prayer, and contemplation. Connecting with nature, spending time in silence, and exploring philosophical or metaphysical teachings can also support the expansion of this chakra.

Remember that working with the chakras is a personal journey, and it is essential to listen to your body and intuition. Regular practice, self-awareness, and a balanced lifestyle can help in harnessing the power of each chakra and promoting overall well-being.

Chapter Nine – Magic in the Americas

Central American and South American cultures, including the Mexicans, Aztecs, Incans, and Mayans, had rich traditions of magic and shamanism that played significant roles in their societies. These ancient civilizations believed in the existence of supernatural forces and spirits that influenced the natural world. Their magical practices and shamanic rituals were deeply rooted in their spiritual beliefs and aimed to maintain harmony between humans, nature, and the divine.

In the worldview of these cultures, magic was seen as a fundamental aspect of life, permeating all existence. It was believed that through the manipulation of these magical forces, shamans and priests could communicate with the spiritual realm and gain insights and guidance for the benefit of their communities. Magic was not seen as something inherently negative or evil but rather as a tool to maintain balance and order in the world.

Shamans, or spiritual leaders, held a central role in these societies. They were highly respected and believed to possess the ability to access the supernatural realms and connect with the spirits. The training of a shaman involved rigorous initiation rituals, often involving solitude, fasting, and visionary experiences induced through the use of psychoactive plants like peyote, ayahuasca, or psilocybin mushrooms. Through these altered states of consciousness, shamans believed they could travel between the realms, communicate with spirits, and gain knowledge and healing powers.

Magic and shamanic practices were employed for various purposes. They were used for healing the sick, divination to predict the future, ensuring successful crops, conducting rituals and ceremonies, and even for military purposes. Rituals and ceremonies were an integral part of these cultures, with offerings made to deities and spirits, and dances and music performed to honor them.

One of the key lessons we can learn from these ancient cultures is the importance of interconnectedness and reverence for the natural world. Central American and South American cultures recognized the deep connection between humans and nature, considering the Earth as a living entity with its own spirit. They understood the significance of maintaining harmony and balance with the environment, and their magical practices reflected this understanding.

Additionally, these cultures valued the wisdom of their ancestors and the spiritual realm. They recognized the role of shamans as intermediaries between the human and spirit worlds, seeking guidance and knowledge from the spiritual realm to benefit their communities. This reverence for ancestral wisdom and spiritual insights can serve as a reminder for us to connect with our own ancestral roots and seek wisdom beyond the material world.

Furthermore, the importance placed on rituals and ceremonies in these cultures highlights the significance of communal activities and shared experiences. These practices brought people together, fostering a sense of belonging and collective identity. In our modern society, where individualism often dominates, we can learn from these cultures' emphasis on communal bonds and the power of shared rituals.

Ultimately, the magical and shamanic practices of the Central American and South American cultures provide insights into the profound spirituality and interconnectedness that permeated their societies. By appreciating and learning from these ancient traditions, we can gain a deeper understanding of our own place in the world and develop a greater sense of respect and harmony with nature and the spiritual realm.

Carlos Castaneda was an influential writer known for his series of books centered around the teachings of a Yaqui Indian shaman named Don Juan Matus. Castaneda's books, beginning with "The Teachings of Don Juan: A Yaqui Way of Knowledge" published in 1968, garnered significant attention and sparked both fascination and controversy.

The themes of Castaneda's books revolved around the exploration of shamanism, indigenous spirituality, and personal transformation. Castaneda portrayed Don Juan as a sorcerer and spiritual guide, describing their encounters and the mystical experiences he underwent under Don Juan's tutelage. Through vivid narratives, Castaneda delved into topics such as altered states of consciousness, sorcery, perception, and the nature of reality.

The lessons imparted by Don Juan in Castaneda's books were often enigmatic and thought-provoking. They emphasized the importance of personal power, the mastery of intent, and the quest for knowledge. Castaneda's works offered a unique perspective on existence, challenging conventional beliefs and inviting readers to question their perception of reality.

Carlos Castaneda's Don Juan books are known for their profound and enigmatic teachings on shamanism and the spiritual journey. Here are some famous quotes from the series:

- "The basic difference between an ordinary man and a warrior is that a warrior takes everything as a challenge, while an ordinary man takes everything as a blessing or a curse." - Don Juan Matus
- "A man of knowledge lives by acting, not by thinking about acting." - Don Juan Matus
- "To achieve the mood of a warrior is not a simple matter. It is a revolution. To regard the lion and the water rats and our fellow men as equals is a magnificent act of a warrior's spirit. It takes power to do that." - Don Juan Matus
- "In the universe, there is an immeasurable, indescribable force which shamans call intent. And absolutely everything that exists in the entire cosmos is attached to intent by a connecting link." - Carlos Castaneda

- "The hardest thing in the world is to assume the mood of a warrior. It is of no use to be sad and complain and feel justified in doing so, believing that someone is always doing something to us. Nobody is doing anything to anybody, much less to a warrior." - Don Juan Matus
- "The average man is hooked to his fellow men, while the warrior is hooked only to infinity." - Don Juan Matus
- "A warrior must cultivate the feeling that he has everything needed for the extravagant journey that is his life. What counts for a warrior is being alive. Life in itself is sufficient, self-explanatory, and complete." - Don Juan Matus
- "For me, a warrior is someone who is outside of himself. A warrior doesn't complain or feel sorry for himself. He understands that everything in life has a purpose, and he is ready to face whatever comes his way." - Don Juan Matus

These quotes capture the essence of the teachings found in Carlos Castaneda's Don Juan books, emphasizing the warrior's mindset, the power of intent, and the pursuit of knowledge and personal transformation.

Regarding historical accuracy, there has been considerable debate and skepticism surrounding Castaneda's accounts. Critics have argued that his books are works of fiction rather than factual documentation. Some skeptics suggest that Castaneda's portrayal of Don Juan was a composite character or even a figment of his imagination. Others claim that Castaneda's narratives were heavily influenced by his own experiences with hallucinogenic substances, such as peyote and psychedelic mushrooms.

The controversy surrounding Castaneda's works stems from several factors. Firstly, critics argue that he did not provide verifiable evidence to support his claims, raising doubts about the authenticity of his experiences. Secondly, some indigenous groups, particularly the Yaqui people, have voiced objections to Castaneda's portrayal of their cultural practices and beliefs. They argued that Castaneda appropriated and distorted their traditions for his own commercial gain.

As for debunking, while the authenticity of Castaneda's accounts remains disputed, several investigations and critiques have emerged over the years. Scholars and researchers have analyzed Castaneda's writings, attempting to separate fact from fiction. Some have accused Castaneda of fabricating events and characters, while others have pointed out inconsistencies and contradictions within his narratives.

It is important to note that Castaneda himself acknowledged that his books were not meant to be taken as straightforward ethnographic or historical records. He often referred to his writings as "anecdotal" or "anthropological fiction." Castaneda maintained that his primary purpose was to convey the essence of Don Juan's teachings and the transformative potential they held.

Carlos Castaneda's books about Don Juan and his teachings were characterized by themes of shamanism, spirituality, and personal transformation. While they captivated readers with their mystical narratives, they also sparked controversy due to questions regarding historical accuracy and accusations of cultural appropriation. Castaneda's works continue to provoke debate and have been subject to critical scrutiny, but they remain influential in the exploration of alternative spiritual perspectives.

Shamans, across various cultures and traditions, have utilized psychoactive plants and mushrooms for spiritual and healing purposes. These plants contain compounds that induce altered states of consciousness, allowing individuals to explore their inner realms, access spiritual dimensions, and gain insights into themselves and the world around them.

While these psychoactive plants have been used by shamans for centuries, it is essential to acknowledge the potential dangers associated with drug use. Misuse or excessive consumption of these substances can lead to physical and psychological harm. The risk of poisoning arises when individuals mistake toxic plants for psychoactive ones or when they consume excessive amounts of psychoactive compounds. This book does not recommend drug use in any way, shape or form because of the dangers involved in experimenting with dangerous compounds that can cause death, mental illness, addiction, and other serious health problems. It is crucial to obtain these plants from reliable sources and under the guidance of experienced practitioners and follow the medical advice of your doctor.

Addiction is a serious concern associated with drug use, including psychoactive plants. While substances like peyote, ayahuasca, and psilocybin mushrooms are not considered addictive in the same way as substances like opioids or stimulants, repeated and irresponsible use can develop into a habitual pattern that may interfere with an individual's daily life and well-being. If you need to use drugs for spiritual purposes, then you should question your motivations. Is it the drugs or the spiritual goals that are your true aspiration? If you are suffering from addiction, you should consult a medical practitioner. There are various drug addiction programs and support groups available in most population centers.

In general, using drugs is considered to be "low magic" as opposed to "high magic". These terms will be explored more in the next chapter but for now, regarding the concept of "low magic," it is important to note that the term itself can have different interpretations depending on the context. In some magical traditions, "low magic" refers to practical magic that focuses on achieving specific outcomes in the physical world. It typically involves the use of rituals, symbols, and herbs, but may not involve altered states of consciousness induced by psychoactive substances.

Using drugs, including psychoactive plants, as a means to access altered states of consciousness or spiritual realms is considered "low magic" because it relies on external substances to facilitate the experience. Some practitioners believe that true spiritual development and magical practice should focus on inner transformation, discipline, and mastery of one's own consciousness, rather than relying on external aids.

However, it's important to note that the perception of "low magic" varies among different magical traditions, and not all practitioners hold the same beliefs. Some may consider working with psychoactive plants as a valid and potent form of spiritual exploration and connection.

Ultimately, it is essential to approach the use of psychoactive plants with caution, respect, and responsible guidance. If someone is interested in exploring their potential benefits, it is advisable to seek out experienced practitioners, adhere to appropriate dosage guidelines, and prioritize safety and personal well-being throughout the journey.

Chapter Ten – High and Low Magic

In the realm of esoteric study, magic is often categorized into two broad categories: high magic and low magic. These terms, however, can have different meanings depending on the magical tradition or practitioner. While there may be general qualities associated with each, it is essential to remember that these concepts are not universally defined and can vary within different magical systems and perspectives.

High Magic: High magic, also known as ceremonial or ritual magic, is often associated with complex rituals, elaborate symbolism, and a focus on spiritual development and transcendence. It places a significant emphasis on structure, discipline, and the use of specific correspondences such as astrology, Kabbalah, and sacred geometry. Practitioners of high magic often work within established magical orders or traditions and follow prescribed rituals with precise gestures, invocations, and invocations.

Qualities of High Magic:
- Complexity: High magic often involves intricate rituals, extensive symbolism, and a deep understanding of esoteric systems.
- Spiritual Focus: It emphasizes spiritual growth, self-transformation, and connection with higher realms or divine forces.
- Discipline and Structure: High magic requires adherence to specific rituals, guidelines, and ethical codes.
- Sacred Knowledge: Practitioners seek to attain wisdom and understanding of the universe's hidden principles and cosmic forces.
- Transcendence: High magic aims to transcend the limitations of the physical realm and explore the realms of the divine and higher consciousness.

One example of High Magic is Kabbalah. This is a mystical and esoteric tradition within Judaism that seeks to explore the nature of God, the universe, and the human soul. It is often referred to as Jewish mysticism and has deep historical and spiritual roots. The word "Kabbalah" itself means "receiving" or "tradition" in Hebrew, indicating its transmission from teacher to student.

The origins of Kabbalah are believed to date back to ancient times, although its exact origins remain uncertain. It developed within Jewish communities in the Middle Ages, primarily in Spain and later in other parts of Europe and the Middle East. Kabbalistic teachings emerged as a response to the desire to gain deeper insight into the mysteries of God and the universe.

Practicing Kabbalah involves a combination of intellectual study, meditation, prayer, and ethical behavior. It delves into complex concepts and symbols to uncover hidden meanings and spiritual truths. Central to Kabbalah is the concept of the Sefirot, which are ten emanations or divine attributes through which God reveals Himself. Understanding and connecting with the Sefirot is a fundamental aspect of Kabbalistic practice.

Kabbalistic teachings encompass various aspects, including cosmology, psychology, meditation techniques, and practical guidance for leading a more spiritual life. It emphasizes the interconnectedness of all things and the idea that everything in the universe contains a divine spark. By exploring and connecting with these divine sparks, individuals can seek to elevate their own spiritual consciousness and bring about positive change in the world.

One of the most well-known texts in Kabbalah is the Zohar, a mystical commentary on the Torah (the Hebrew Bible) attributed to Rabbi Shimon bar Yochai. The Zohar provides deep insights into the nature of God, the creation of the universe, and the spiritual dimensions of reality.

Kabbalah teaches that each person has the potential to connect with the divine and achieve spiritual enlightenment. It offers tools and practices to help individuals develop a deeper understanding of themselves and their relationship with God. Kabbalistic study and contemplation aim to expand consciousness, foster personal growth, and promote a sense of unity and harmony with the universe.

Furthermore, Kabbalah places importance on ethical behavior and moral conduct. It emphasizes the cultivation of virtues such as compassion, love, and justice. The teachings of Kabbalah encourage individuals to use their spiritual insights and knowledge to bring about positive change in their lives and in society as a whole.

In summary, Kabbalah is a mystical tradition within Judaism that explores the nature of God, the universe, and the human soul. Through a combination of intellectual study, meditation, prayer, and ethical behavior, practitioners seek to deepen their spiritual connection, gain insights into the mysteries of existence, and bring about positive transformation in themselves and the world around them.

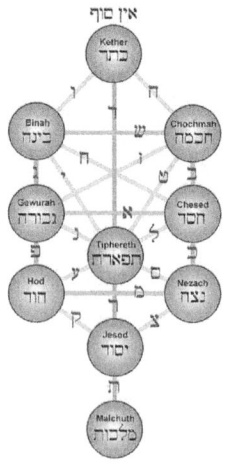

Another example of high magic is sacred geometry. This try refers to the study of geometric principles and patterns that are believed to have deep spiritual or symbolic significance. It explores the interrelationship between geometry, mathematics, and the underlying structure of the universe. Proponents of sacred geometry argue that these geometric forms can be found in nature, architecture, and religious or spiritual symbols and that they hold inherent beauty and meaning.

Sacred geometry has roots in various ancient civilizations, including Egyptian, Greek, and Islamic cultures. Many ancient cultures considered geometry as a pathway to understanding the divine and believed that certain geometric shapes held mystical properties. The Pythagoreans, a school of ancient Greek philosophers, regarded geometry as the key to unlocking the secrets of the universe.

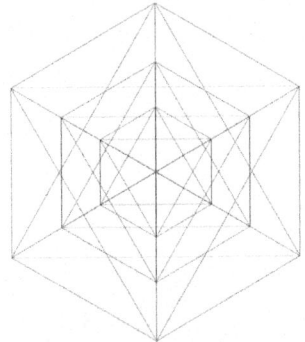

The evidence for sacred geometry lies in its prevalence across diverse cultures and time periods. Numerous examples can be found in architecture, art, and religious symbols throughout history. For instance, the Great Pyramid of Giza in Egypt showcases precise geometric alignments and proportions. The use of geometric patterns in Islamic architecture, such as in mosques and palaces, is another example. Additionally, the intricate geometrical designs found in mandalas, yantras, and other spiritual symbols from various traditions are considered manifestations of sacred geometry.

Sacred geometry can be observed in the natural world as well. The spirals found in seashells and sunflowers, the hexagonal patterns of honeycombs, and the logarithmic spiral of a nautilus shell are often cited as examples of sacred geometry in nature. Moreover, the geometric relationships and ratios found in the human body, such as the Golden Ratio, are believed by some to be manifestations of sacred geometry.

Famous Authors: Several authors have written extensively on the subject of sacred geometry. Notable figures include:

- Pythagoras: The ancient Greek philosopher who emphasized the role of geometry in understanding the cosmos.
- Plato: The Greek philosopher who explored the concept of ideal forms and the relationship between geometry and reality.
- Johannes Kepler: The German mathematician and astronomer who linked geometry and planetary motion.
- Drunvalo Melchizedek: Known for his work on the Flower of Life, Merkaba, and sacred geometry in the context of spiritual evolution.
- Robert Lawlor: An author who has written on the interconnections between sacred geometry, cosmology, and ancient cultures.

Studying sacred geometry can offer several lessons and insights. It can foster an appreciation for the inherent harmony and order in the universe. It reminds us of the interconnectedness of all things and encourages a holistic perspective. Sacred geometry can also inspire creativity, as it provides a framework for understanding and creating aesthetically pleasing and balanced designs. Additionally, it invites contemplation on the relationship between the material and the spiritual, as well as the underlying patterns that govern existence.

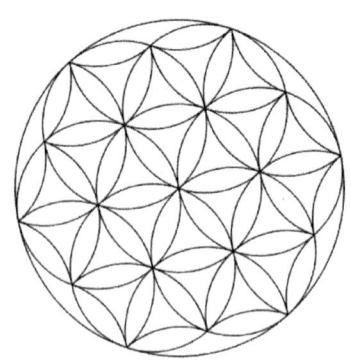

Low Magic: Low magic, also referred to as folk or practical magic, is generally associated with more accessible and everyday forms of magical practice. It focuses on practical goals, such as healing, protection, divination, and influencing everyday events. Low magic can be found in various cultural traditions and often incorporates folk remedies, charms, talismans, and simple rituals.

Qualities of Low Magic:

- Practicality: Low magic aims to address practical concerns and everyday needs, such as love, health, and prosperity.
- Simplicity: It relies on accessible tools and techniques, often passed down through generations and grounded in folk traditions.
- Intuitive Approach: Low magic places importance on personal intuition and working with one's immediate environment.
- Empowerment: Practitioners of low magic seek to empower themselves and others through the manipulation of energies and forces.
- Cultural Adaptation: Low magic often reflects the cultural beliefs, practices, and folklore of a particular region or community.

Traditional folk magic is given as an example of low magic. Folk magic, also known as traditional or folkloric magic, refers to a broad range of magical practices that have been passed down through generations within specific cultural or regional communities. Rooted in the beliefs, customs, and traditions of ordinary people, folk magic encompasses various forms of divination, healing, protection, and spellcasting. These practices often rely on the use of natural materials, such as herbs, stones, candles, and charms, and involve rituals and incantations.

Folk magic varies greatly across different cultures and regions, each with its own unique set of beliefs and practices. Here are a few examples of traditional folk magic from various parts of the world:

Hoodoo: Originating in the African American community, particularly in the Southern United States, Hoodoo incorporates elements of African spirituality, Native American traditions, and European folk magic. Hoodoo practitioners use herbs, roots, oils, candles, and amulets to cast spells for purposes such as love, luck, protection, and uncrossing.

European Witchcraft: Traditional witchcraft in Europe encompasses a wide range of magical practices. For instance, in the British Isles, practitioners of witchcraft may use charms, herbs, and divination techniques to heal ailments, ward off evil spirits, or foretell the future. The Cunning Folk of England were renowned for their abilities in folk magic, offering services like spellcasting, healing, and protection.

Brujería: Brujería, meaning "witchcraft" in Spanish, is a form of folk magic prevalent in Latin American cultures, particularly in Mexico and Central America. Brujos and brujas (male and female practitioners, respectively) employ a combination of herbal remedies, prayers, candle magic, and spirit work to address issues such as love, prosperity, protection, and hex removal.

Appalachian Folk Magic: Rooted in the mountainous regions of the southeastern United States, Appalachian folk magic incorporates elements from various cultural influences, including Native American, African, and European traditions. Practices may involve using natural objects like stones, feathers, and plants for divination, protection, and healing purposes.

Norse Seidr: Seidr, an ancient form of Norse magic, was predominantly practiced by women known as seidkonur. They used rituals, trance work, and divination to connect with spirits and deities, seeking knowledge, healing, and influencing events. Seidr encompassed both practical and mystical aspects of life and played a significant role in Norse mythology and folklore.

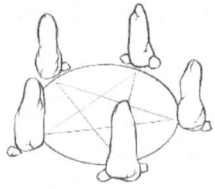

It's important to note that folk magic is deeply tied to specific cultural contexts and beliefs. While these examples provide a glimpse into the diverse world of folk magic, each culture and community will have its own unique practices and traditions.

Similarities between high and low magic: Intention and Willpower: Both high and low magic rely on the practitioner's focused intention and willpower to direct and manifest their desired outcomes.

Connection to the Mystical: Both forms of magic recognize the existence of a hidden or unseen world beyond the physical realm and seek to tap into its energies and forces.

Personal Transformation: While their approaches may differ, both high and low magic can facilitate personal growth, expanded consciousness, and a deeper understanding of oneself and the universe.

Which One is Better? Determining which form of magic is "better" is subjective and depends on the individual practitioner's goals, beliefs, and preferences. High magic may appeal to those seeking a structured and disciplined approach to spiritual development, esoteric knowledge, and transcendence. On the other hand, low magic may be more appealing to those interested in practical outcomes, folk traditions, and a connection to their cultural heritage. Ultimately, the effectiveness and fulfillment derived from magic are deeply personal, and each practitioner should explore what resonates with them on their own magical journey.

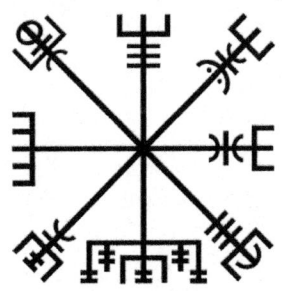

Chapter Eleven – Indigenous Magic

When looking for different wizards and magicians all over the world, it is easy to see that there is a wide range of examples from all the corners of the globe and amongst all its many peoples. As such, it is impossible to give each of these vibrant cultures and traditions the detailed attention that they deserve. However, any serious aspirant looking to broaden their understanding of these magnificent cultures would be well-rewarded for exploring these wonderful, ancient traditions.

Polynesian Folk Magic:
Polynesian folk magic refers to the traditional magical practices and beliefs found in the Polynesian islands, including Hawaii, Samoa, Tonga, Tahiti, and Māori culture in New Zealand. Here are some key aspects:

Mana: Central to Polynesian magic is the concept of mana, a spiritual force or power that exists in all things. Mana can be harnessed and manipulated by individuals with special knowledge or abilities.

Kahuna: In Hawaiian culture, a kahuna is a practitioner who acts as a spiritual guide and healer. They possess extensive knowledge of herbs, rituals, chants, and spells to bring about healing, protection, and other desired outcomes.

Hula and Chants: Hula, a traditional Hawaiian dance, is often associated with magical and spiritual practices. Chants and songs, known as mele, are performed during rituals to connect with ancestral spirits and invoke their power.

Tikis and Totems: Carvings of tikis (humanoid figures) and totems hold significant spiritual importance in Polynesian culture. They are believed to house protective spirits or deities and are used in rituals for blessings and spiritual connection.

The Māori people are the indigenous Polynesian population of New Zealand. They have a rich cultural heritage that includes a variety of folk beliefs and traditions. Māori folklore and spirituality are deeply intertwined with their everyday lives and encompass a wide range of beliefs about the supernatural, including magic.

Magic, or "mākutu" in the Māori language, is an integral part of traditional Māori beliefs. It refers to the use of supernatural powers and practices to influence or control various aspects of life. Māori magic is often seen as a manifestation of spiritual power and is closely tied to the concept of "mana," which refers to a person's spiritual energy or authority.

In Māori belief, magic can be both positive and negative. We will talk more about black and white magic in following chapters but for now, the Māori belief in positive and negative magic gives an interesting segway into this discussion. Positive magic, known as "mākutu whakapai," is used for healing, protection, and enhancing spiritual well-being. This includes practices such as herbal remedies, incantations, and rituals performed by tohunga (spiritual experts or healers). These tohunga possess specialized knowledge and skills passed down through generations, enabling them to connect with the spiritual realm and channel positive energies for the benefit of individuals and the community.

On the other hand, negative magic, known as "mākutu whiwhi," involves the use of supernatural powers to harm others. It is often associated with witchcraft or sorcery and is believed to be driven by envy, anger, or other negative emotions. Māori folklore contains tales of individuals who were believed to have possessed dark powers and used them to inflict illness, misfortune, or even death upon others. The effects of negative magic were considered real and believed to have significant consequences on the target.

To address instances of negative magic, Māori communities employed various protective measures. These could include rituals, charms, or talismans to ward off evil influences and counteract the effects of mākutu. Additionally, spiritual leaders and tohunga would often perform ceremonies and prayers to cleanse and restore balance within the affected individuals or communities.

It's important to note that Māori beliefs and practices vary among different iwi (tribes) and regions, and not all Māori individuals or communities may adhere to these traditional beliefs and practices in the same way. Over time, the influence of Christianity and Western culture has also shaped the Māori worldview and led to a blending of traditional and contemporary beliefs.

Today, while some Māori continue to engage with traditional beliefs and practices, many also practice other religions or hold diverse spiritual beliefs. Māori cultural revitalization efforts have led to a renewed interest in traditional knowledge, including magic, and its integration into modern Māori identity and cultural expression.

Australian Aboriginal Folk Magic:

Australian Indigenous people are the original inhabitants of the Australian continent and its nearby islands. They are one of the world's oldest living cultures, with a rich history that dates back at least 65,000 years. This makes their culture one of the oldest continuous cultures on Earth.

Before the arrival of European settlers in 1788, Australian Indigenous people lived in diverse and complex societies, with distinct languages, customs, and spiritual beliefs. They consisted of hundreds of different tribal and language groups, each with their own unique traditions and practices. Despite this diversity, there were some commonalities in their ways of life.

The Indigenous people of Australia were primarily hunter-gatherers, relying on the abundant natural resources of the land, waterways, and oceans. They had a deep understanding of the local environment and its seasons, which enabled them to navigate and survive in diverse ecosystems ranging from deserts to rainforests. Their hunting techniques included the use of spears, boomerangs, and other tools while gathering involved collecting various plants, fruits, and seeds.

Indigenous communities were generally organized around kinship systems, with family and clan connections forming the basis of social structures. Elders held significant roles as custodians of knowledge, passing down cultural traditions, stories, and laws through oral histories and teachings. These traditions played a vital role in maintaining social order and ensuring the well-being of the community.

The connection to the land is fundamental to Indigenous Australian cultures. They have a spiritual and ancestral connection to their traditional lands, known as "Country." For Indigenous people, Country is not merely a physical place but also a spiritual entity that encompasses their entire worldview, culture, and identity. The land is believed to be created and shaped by ancestral beings during the Dreaming or Creation Time, and Indigenous people see themselves as custodians of the land, with a responsibility to care for and protect it.

Indigenous Australians have a profound understanding of the natural environment and its interconnectedness with all living beings. Their knowledge includes detailed observations of plants, animals, and natural phenomena, as well as sustainable land management practices that have been refined over thousands of years.

Indigenous cultural practices, such as ceremonies, rituals, and art, are often deeply rooted in the connection to the land. These practices serve to strengthen the spiritual ties between people, ancestors, and Country. Aboriginal and Torres Strait Islander art, with its distinctive symbols and styles, often depicts stories of the Dreaming, cultural histories, and the relationship between humans and the land.

Despite the significant impacts of colonization and ongoing challenges faced by Indigenous communities, the cultural traditions, languages, and connection to the land remain strong and continue to be celebrated and revitalized by Indigenous Australians today.

Australian Aboriginal folk magic encompasses the mystical practices of Indigenous Australian cultures. Here are some notable features:

Dreamtime: The concept of Dreamtime is central to Aboriginal spirituality. It refers to the mythical time of creation when ancestral beings shaped the land, animals, and people. Magical rituals and stories are often connected to Dreamtime.

Songlines: Songlines, also known as Dreaming tracks, are paths across the land that trace the journeys of ancestral beings. These songs and stories contain sacred knowledge, and through song and dance, they connect the present generation with ancestral spirits.

Bush Medicine: Aboriginal folk magic includes a deep understanding of bush medicine, using plants and natural remedies for healing physical and spiritual ailments. The knowledge of medicinal plants is passed down through generations.

Rituals and Ceremonies: Aboriginal rituals and ceremonies involve dances, music, body paintings, and the recitation of sacred stories. These practices aim to maintain the balance between the spiritual and physical realms, ensuring the well-being of individuals and the community.

Southeast Asian Folk Magic:

Often, when we think of Southeast Asia, we think about the cultural influences of China, India, and Islam on the region. When we think of the people themselves, we draw upon the readily available information and representation of the dominant peoples of that region. However, within the many different peoples and cultures of Southeast Asia, are many indigenous tribes, who strive to preserve their traditional ways of life. They may not have a country of their own, or indeed, they may have tribal group members living in different countries as their traditional lands cross borders. However, their stories are important to the multifaceted jewel that is Southeast Asia.

Southeast Asian folk magic encompasses a diverse range of magical practices found in countries such as Thailand, Indonesia, Malaysia, the Philippines, and Cambodia. Here are some common elements:

Shamanism: Shamanic practices play a significant role in Southeast Asian folk magic. Shamanic practitioners, known as bomohs (Malaysia), dukuns (Indonesia), or babaylans (Philippines), communicate with spirits and perform healing, divination, and protection rituals.

Talismans and Amulets: Talismans and amulets are prevalent in Southeast Asian folk magic. They are believed to possess protective and magical properties and are often worn or carried for various purposes, such as warding off evil spirits, bringing luck, or enhancing personal power.

Ancestor Worship: Ancestor veneration is common in Southeast Asian cultures. Rituals and offerings are made to ancestors to seek their guidance and blessings. This practice involves honoring ancestral spirits and seeking their intervention in daily life.

Magic Spells and Incantations: Magical spells and incantations are used in Southeast Asian folk magic to invoke deities, spirits, or supernatural forces. These spells can be chanted, written, or performed in rituals to achieve specific outcomes, such as love, protection, or prosperity.

It's important to note that folk magic practices can vary within these regions due to cultural diversity and local variations. These practices are deeply rooted in the cultural and spiritual traditions of the respective communities and continue to be an integral part of their heritage.

Chapter Twelve – Black, White, and Gray Magic

Black, gray, and white magic are terms often used to categorize different forms of magical practices and intentions. While these terms are subjective and can vary in meaning across different cultural and magical traditions, I can provide a general overview of their qualities and how they are commonly perceived to be different.

Black Magic: Black magic is generally associated with practices that involve the use of supernatural forces or energies for negative or harmful purposes. It is often characterized by the intention to manipulate or control others, inflict harm, or bring about negative outcomes. Black magic is typically seen as unethical or morally wrong, as it goes against the principles of free will and causes harm to others. Spells or rituals associated with black magic may involve curses, hexes, or malicious intent.

Gray Magic: Gray magic falls in the middle ground between black and white magic, encompassing practices that are neither completely negative nor entirely positive. It is often associated with neutrality, balance, and working with both light and dark energies. Gray magic practitioners may employ their skills for various purposes, including protection, personal growth, or helping others, but their methods may not always conform to strict moral guidelines. Gray magic acknowledges the existence of duality and the potential for both positive and negative outcomes.

White Magic: White magic is generally associated with practices that involve the use of supernatural forces or energies for positive and beneficial purposes. It is often characterized by intentions such as healing, protection, personal growth, or promoting harmony and well-being. White magic practitioners typically adhere to ethical guidelines, respecting the principles of free will and avoiding harm to others. Spells or rituals associated with white magic may involve healing, blessings, or spells aimed at attracting positive energies.

It is important to note that the classification of magic into black, gray, and white is not universally agreed upon and can vary depending on cultural, religious, or personal beliefs. Some magical traditions may not use these terms at all, while others may have different categorizations altogether. The interpretation and usage of these terms can differ among individuals and communities, so it's always essential to consider the specific context and cultural background when discussing magic.

In general, the attributes of white, gray, and black magic can be summarized as follows:

White Magic:

Healing: A healer using herbs, energy work, or spiritual practices to aid in physical and emotional well-being.

Protection: Creating wards or casting spells to safeguard individuals or places from harm.

Blessings: Performing rituals to bring good fortune, abundance, or positive energy to a person or situation.

Black Magic:

Curses: Casting spells or rituals with the intention of causing harm, misfortune, or illness to others.

Necromancy: Communicating with or manipulating spirits or the dead for personal gain or malicious purposes.

Dark Summoning: Invoking dark entities or forces to carry out one's bidding or gain power over others.

Gray Magic:

Divination: Using tools like tarot cards or crystal balls to gain insight into the future or receive guidance.

Manipulation: Influencing people or situations through magical means, but without causing direct harm.

Binding: Restricting or containing someone or something's power or influence to prevent harm or misuse.

Representations of gray, white and black magic:

In movies and literature, the portrayal of white, gray, and black magicians can vary depending on the story and its context. Here are some common depictions:

White Magicians:

Pure-hearted Heroes: Often portrayed as wise, benevolent figures using their powers for the greater good, such as Gandalf from "The Lord of the Rings" or Dumbledore from the "Harry Potter" series.

Healing Characters: Often depicted as nurturing and compassionate individuals, like the White Witch in C.S. Lewis's "The Chronicles of Narnia."

Nature-oriented Practitioners: Shown as having a deep connection with nature and using magic to protect and preserve it, such as the elves in J.R.R. Tolkien's works.

Black Magicians:

Villains and Antagonists: Frequently portrayed as malicious, power-hungry individuals who use dark magic for personal gain or to cause harm, like Lord Voldemort in the "Harry Potter" series or the Wicked Witch of the West in "The Wizard of Oz."

Corrupted Heroes: Sometimes depicted as characters who started with good intentions but became corrupted by the allure of dark magic, as seen in Anakin Skywalker's transformation into Darth Vader in "Star Wars."

Cultists or Dark Sorcerers: Represented as members of secret societies or individuals who delve into forbidden knowledge, summoning demons, or performing rituals for nefarious purposes.

Gray Magicians:

Mystical Mentors: Often portrayed as enigmatic characters who guide the protagonist on their journey, providing mystical knowledge and insight, like Obi-Wan Kenobi in "Star Wars."

Ambiguous Characters: Sometimes depicted as morally complex figures who use magic to serve their own interests, neither purely good nor evil.

Tricksters or Cunning Sorcerers: Shown as characters who use their magical abilities for mischief, personal gain, or to teach valuable lessons, such as Merlin in Arthurian legends or Loki in Norse mythology.

Chapter Thirteen – Magic of Different Colors

In various magical systems and belief systems, different colors are often associated with specific energies, symbolism, and meanings. While the interpretations and associations of colors can vary, here's a general explanation of magic from different colors:

Red Magic:
Red magic is often associated with passion, courage, strength, and vitality. It embodies the fiery and energetic aspects of magic. Red magic can be used for love spells, enhancing personal power, increasing motivation, and boosting physical energy. It may also help with assertiveness and protection. The lessons offered by red magic revolve around embracing passion, taking action, and channeling emotions effectively.

Green Magic:
Green magic is closely tied to nature, growth, abundance, and healing. It taps into the energy of plants, forests, and the natural world. Green magic can be used for spells related to fertility, prosperity, herbalism, and connecting with the Earth's energies. It encourages a deep appreciation for nature, environmental stewardship, and the cycles of life. The lessons offered by green magic revolve around harmony, balance, and nurturing connections with the natural world.

Yellow Magic:
Yellow magic is associated with intellect, communication, creativity, and clarity. It encompasses the qualities of joy, optimism, and mental stimulation. Yellow magic can be used for spells related to enhancing communication skills, boosting confidence, increasing mental focus, and promoting creativity. It encourages positive thinking, mental expansion, and self-expression. The lessons offered by yellow magic revolve around embracing intellect, seeking knowledge, and expressing oneself authentically.

Purple Magic:
Purple magic is often connected with spirituality, intuition, mysticism, and transformation. It represents the merging of the physical and spiritual

realms. Purple magic can be used for spells related to psychic abilities, spiritual development, meditation, and accessing higher realms of consciousness. It encourages introspection, inner wisdom, and spiritual growth. The lessons offered by purple magic revolve around developing intuition, exploring the depths of the self, and embracing spiritual connection.

Blue Magic:

Blue magic is associated with calmness, serenity, healing, and emotional well-being. It embodies the qualities of peace, tranquility, and soothing energies. Blue magic can be used for spells related to emotional healing, stress reduction, communication, and promoting harmony in relationships. It encourages emotional balance, introspection, and self-reflection. The lessons offered by blue magic revolve around finding inner peace, embracing emotional healing, and fostering harmonious connections with others.

Brown Magic:

Brown magic is closely tied to stability, grounding, and practicality. It represents the solid and earthy aspects of magic. Brown magic can be used for spells related to stability, home and hearth, grounding, and practical matters. It encourages a sense of security, practicality, and a connection with the physical world. The lessons offered by brown magic revolve around building a strong foundation, embracing simplicity, and finding stability in one's life.

Pink Magic:

Pink magic is associated with love, compassion, harmony, and emotional healing. It embodies the gentle and nurturing aspects of magic. Pink magic can be used for spells related to self-love, attracting love and friendship, healing emotional wounds, and fostering compassion. It encourages a loving and caring approach to oneself and others. The lessons offered by pink magic revolve around practicing self-love, cultivating empathy, and fostering harmonious relationships.

Orange Magic:

Orange magic is often connected with enthusiasm, creativity, joy, and abundance. It represents the energies of warmth, vitality, and optimism.

Orange magic can be used for spells related to creativity, motivation, inspiration, and attracting abundance in various areas of life. It encourages a zest for life, embracing new experiences, and embracing positive change. The lessons offered by orange magic revolve around embracing enthusiasm, cultivating creativity, and seeking joy.

Indigo Magic:

Indigo magic is associated with spirituality, intuition, psychic abilities, and higher consciousness. It represents the deep and mystical aspects of magic. Indigo magic can be used for spells related to psychic development, spiritual insight, divination, and connecting with the unseen realms. It encourages a deeper understanding of the spiritual self and the exploration of higher realms of consciousness. The lessons offered by indigo magic revolve around trusting intuition, exploring the mysteries of the universe, and embracing spiritual wisdom.

It's important to note that these associations can vary across different magical traditions, cultures, and individual practitioners. The interpretation and practice of magic are highly personal and can differ based on individual beliefs and experiences.

Chapter Fourteen – Ceremonial Magic

Ceremonial magic, also known as high magic or ritual magic, is a system of magical practice that traces its origins back to ancient times. Its roots can be found in the magical traditions of ancient Egypt, Mesopotamia, Greece, and the Jewish mystical tradition of Kabbalah. Ceremonial magic gained prominence during the European Renaissance, particularly through the works of figures like Heinrich Cornelius Agrippa, Marsilio Ficino, and the Hermetic Order of the Golden Dawn.

This form of magic emphasizes the precise execution of rituals, the use of complex symbols and correspondences, and the invocation of divine or spiritual entities. Ceremonial magicians often work within a structured framework, following specific rituals and ceremonial procedures. The intention is to establish a connection with higher powers, attain spiritual knowledge, and harness supernatural forces for personal transformation or magical workings.

In many religions, ceremonies play a significant role in worship and spiritual practices. The Catholic Church, for example, has a rich tradition of elaborate ceremonies and rituals. Some common ceremonies observed in the Catholic Church include:

Mass: The central act of Catholic worship, where the Eucharist (Holy Communion) is celebrated. It involves prayers, readings from the Bible, the consecration of bread and wine, and the distribution of the Eucharistic elements to the faithful.

Baptism: The sacrament of initiation into the Christian faith, which involves the pouring or immersion of water over a person's head, accompanied by prayers and blessings.

Confirmation: A sacrament where individuals receive the Holy Spirit through anointing with oil by a bishop. It signifies a deeper commitment to the Christian faith and the empowerment to live as a fully initiated member of the Church.

Marriage: A sacred union between a man and a woman, where the couple exchange vows before a priest and witnesses. It is accompanied by prayers, blessings, and the exchange of rings.

Last Rites: A set of prayers and sacraments administered to the dying or seriously ill, including the Sacrament of the Anointing of the Sick and Viaticum (reception of Holy Communion).

These ceremonies in the Catholic Church are designed to facilitate a connection with the divine, invoke blessings, and provide a framework for communal worship and spiritual growth.

It's important to note that magical rituals and ceremonies can vary significantly across cultures, belief systems, and individual practices. The specific tools, symbols, and rituals used can differ based on personal preferences, traditions, and intended outcomes.

Magical rituals and ceremonies have been an integral part of human history, spanning across various cultures and belief systems. These practices involve a combination of symbolic actions, invocations, and focused intention to tap into supernatural forces or higher realms of consciousness. While the specifics of magical rituals can vary widely, there are certain common elements and tools used in many traditions.

In magical rituals, practitioners often create a sacred space, such as a consecrated circle, to establish a connection with the spiritual realm. This can be done using various tools and objects that hold symbolic meaning. An example of this can be found in modern Wicca or witchcraft. Some commonly used items for their rituals include:

Altar: A dedicated surface used to hold ritual objects, symbols, and offerings. It serves as a focal point for the practitioner's intention and devotion.

Candles: Lit candles are often employed to represent the presence of light, purity, and spiritual energy. Different colored candles may be used to correspond with specific intentions or elemental energies.

Incense: Fragrant herbs and resins are burned as offerings or to purify the ritual space. The smoke is believed to carry prayers and intentions to the spiritual realm.

Athame: A ceremonial knife or dagger, often with a double-edged blade, which symbolizes the practitioner's will and the ability to direct energy. It is typically used for drawing energy, casting circles, and invoking or banishing forces.

Wand: A wand represents the element of air and is used to direct and focus magical energy. It is commonly associated with invocation and manifestation.

Chalice: A sacred cup or goblet that holds water or other ritual beverages. It represents the element of water and is used for libations and ceremonial sharing.

Pentacle: A flat disc or plate inscribed with symbols, often including the pentagram, which represents the integration of the elements and the divine. It serves as a sacred space for consecration and charging of objects.

Book of Shadows: A personal journal or grimoire where practitioners record their rituals, spells, correspondences, and spiritual experiences. It acts as a guide and repository of magical knowledge.

The Hermetic Order of the Golden Dawn

This was a magical order that emerged during the late 19th century. It was founded in London, England, in 1888 by three prominent occultists: William Robert Woodman, William Wynn Westcott, and Samuel Liddell MacGregor Mathers. The Golden Dawn sought to explore and practice various occult and esoteric teachings, drawing from a wide range of spiritual and mystical traditions.

The Golden Dawn's belief system incorporated elements from Hermeticism, Qabalah, astrology, alchemy, Tarot, and ceremonial magic. They viewed the universe as a vast interconnected web of energies and sought to understand and manipulate these forces through ritual and symbolic practices. Central to their philosophy was the pursuit of spiritual growth, self-transformation, and the attainment of divine knowledge.

The order held a belief in a hierarchical structure of existence, with different realms or planes of existence, each associated with specific divine and spiritual forces. These forces were represented by various deities, angels, and spiritual beings. The Golden Dawn sought to establish contact with these forces through ceremonial rituals, meditation, and the use of magical tools and symbols.

The Golden Dawn's rituals and ceremonies were designed to facilitate spiritual development, inner transformation, and the exploration of occult mysteries. They employed elaborate and symbolic rituals that drew upon ancient Egyptian, Greek, and Hebrew traditions. The order's rituals were typically performed in a group setting and involved the use of ceremonial robes, magical tools, and incantations.

One of the key rituals of the Golden Dawn was the Lesser Banishing Ritual of the Pentagram, which was used for purification and protection. This ritual involved visualizing and tracing pentagrams in the air while invoking divine names and forces associated with the four elements.

The Golden Dawn also utilized a series of initiation ceremonies that marked the progress and advancement of its members through different grades or degrees within the order. These initiations were secretive and involved oath-bound rituals, symbolic tests, and the transmission of esoteric teachings.

The Hermetic Order of the Golden Dawn attracted many notable individuals who played significant roles in the occult and esoteric movements of the time. Some famous practitioners associated with the Golden Dawn include:

Aleister Crowley: An influential occultist, writer, and ceremonial magician, Crowley joined the Golden Dawn in the late 1890s and later became involved in a power struggle within the order. He went on to found his own magical order, the A∴A∴.

W.B. Yeats: The renowned Irish poet and playwright, W.B. Yeats, was a member of the Golden Dawn. He drew inspiration from his occult studies and incorporated esoteric symbolism and themes into his literary works.

Dion Fortune: A British occultist and author, Dion Fortune studied with the Golden Dawn and went on to establish her own magical group, the Fraternity of the Inner Light. She wrote extensively on occult topics and is known for her novel "The Sea Priestess."

Florence Farr: An actress and occultist, Farr was a prominent figure within the Golden Dawn and played a key role in its development. She contributed to the order's rituals and teachings and was an advocate for women's involvement in occult practices.

It is worth noting that the Golden Dawn experienced internal conflicts and eventually dissolved in the early 20th century. However, its teachings and influence have left a lasting impact on modern Western occultism, and many of its concepts and practices continue to be studied and utilized by contemporary magical and esoteric practitioners.

Chapter Fifteen – Right-hand Path vs. Left-hand Path

The concepts of the left-hand path and right-hand path originate from various mystical and occult traditions and have been used to describe different approaches to magic and spiritual practices. While these terms can have multiple interpretations depending on the context, Here is a general overview of their philosophies and some notable figures associated with each path.

The Right-Hand Path: The right-hand path is often associated with traditions that emphasize moral and ethical codes, and the pursuit of spiritual enlightenment through self-discipline and adherence to established societal norms. Practitioners on this path typically seek union with the divine or a higher power and strive to align their actions with principles such as compassion, altruism, and selflessness. They tend to view magic as a tool for personal growth, healing, and spiritual development within the boundaries of accepted social norms.

Famous Figures Associated with the Right-Hand Path:

Aleister Crowley: Although Crowley is known for his association with both paths, he initially leaned more towards the right-hand path in his early life. He later developed his own system called Thelema, which incorporates elements of both paths.

Dion Fortune: A British occultist and writer who advocated for the responsible use of occult knowledge and emphasized the integration of magic with psychological development.

Gerald Gardner: Regarded as the founder of modern Wicca, Gardner emphasized ethical practices, reverence for nature, and the concept of "harm none" in his form of witchcraft.

The Left-Hand Path: The left-hand path is often associated with more unconventional and individualistic approaches to spirituality and magic. Practitioners on this path may reject or challenge established moral and societal norms, seeking personal power, self-deification, and liberation from traditional restrictions. They may embrace aspects of darkness, explore taboo subjects, and actively engage with their own desires and ego. The left-hand path is often seen as a more transgressive and rebellious approach to magic and spiritual exploration.

Famous Figures Associated with the Left-Hand Path:

Eliphas Levi: A 19th-century French occultist who explored the concept of divine magic and the union of opposites. Although not exclusively associated with the left-hand path, his works had a considerable influence on its development.

Anton LaVey: The founder of the Church of Satan, LaVey emphasized individualism, rational self-interest, and the pursuit of personal gratification. He rejected supernatural beliefs and advocated for the symbolic use of magic.

Michael W. Ford: An author and practitioner of left-hand path traditions, Ford has written extensively on assorted topics related to the left-hand path, including demonic magic and self-deification.

It's important to note that these descriptions provide a general understanding of the left-hand path and right-hand path. However, the philosophies and practices associated with these paths can vary significantly depending on the specific traditions, cultures, and individuals involved.

Cautionary Statement: The Occult and Its Risks

Engaging with alternative spiritual paths, such as the Left-Hand Path, can be enticing to some individuals seeking unique perspectives and experiences. However, it is crucial to approach such paths with caution and awareness of the potential dangers involved. There are three significant concerns associated with involvement in practices centered around demon worship, devil worship, self-gratification, and cults: spiritual harm, ethical pitfalls, and the risk of sexual abuse.

Spiritual Harm: Embracing the Left-Hand Path often involves interacting with entities associated with darkness, demons, or malevolent forces. While some may believe they can control or harness these energies, it is essential to understand the inherent risks. Engaging with darker energies (whether they be real or imagined) can have profound and lasting effects on one's spiritual well-being and mental health. It may lead to spiritual imbalance, mental distress, and emotional turmoil. The pursuit of power and control over these forces can result in personal spiritual corruption, creating long-term consequences that are challenging to reverse.

Ethical Pitfalls: Many practices associated with the Left-Hand Path prioritize self-gratification, personal power, and the pursuit of individual desires without considering the consequences for others. Surrounding oneself with individuals who follow a selfish path can lead to a toxic environment and a disregard for ethical principles. This can harm relationships, contribute to social isolation, and erode one's sense of empathy and compassion. It is crucial to consider the broader impact of our actions and decisions, both on ourselves and the world around us.

Cults and Sexual Abuse: Within certain occult or esoteric circles, there may be groups that masquerade as spiritual communities while engaging in manipulative or abusive practices. Sexual abuse is a deeply troubling issue that can occur within these settings. Cults may exploit vulnerable individuals, using their desires for spiritual growth and connection to exert control and perpetrate harm. It is essential to be vigilant and aware of the signs of manipulation, coercion, and abuse within any spiritual or occult group.

In summary, exploring the Left-Hand Path or engaging with people who claim to worship demons, or the devil requires careful consideration and discernment. While it is possible to pursue alternative spiritual paths responsibly, it is crucial to remain aware of the potential risks involved. These risks include spiritual harm, ethical pitfalls, and the potential for sexual abuse within certain cultic environments. It is advisable to approach these paths with a critical mindset, prioritize personal well-being, and seek guidance from trustworthy sources to ensure one's safety and spiritual growth. Never become involved in a group that seeks to isolate you from your friends or family or asks you to do anything that makes you feel uncomfortable or engages in illegal or immoral activities.

Chapter Sixteen – Skeptics and Frauds

Skeptics generally approach magic and wizardry with a skeptical mindset, questioning the existence and validity of such phenomena. They often argue that magic and wizardry are simply products of illusion, trickery, or a lack of understanding about natural phenomena. Skeptics may argue that claims of magic are based on anecdotal evidence, subjective experiences, or cultural beliefs rather than scientific inquiry.

To date, there is no scientifically accepted evidence that demonstrates the existence of magic in the literal sense. The scientific method, which relies on empirical observation, experimentation, and replication, has not been able to validate magical claims. The absence of verifiable evidence is a significant factor leading skeptics to doubt the existence of magic.

Many people have attempted to prove the existence of magic throughout history, but their efforts have largely been met with skepticism or debunked by scientific scrutiny. Researchers and magicians have often investigated claims of supernatural abilities or magical powers, but rigorous scientific examination has generally failed to support these claims.

It's worth noting that some forms of magic, such as stage magic or illusionism, are recognized as entertainment and performance art rather than supernatural occurrences. These forms of magic rely on misdirection, sleight of hand, and other techniques to create the illusion of extraordinary events. While they can be impressive and captivating, they are not considered evidence of supernatural or magical powers.

Ultimately, the existence of magic and wizardry remains a topic of debate and skepticism among rational thinkers and scientists who require empirical evidence to accept extraordinary claims.

Unfortunately, people of dubious intent have employed various techniques to deceive others into believing they possess magical or divine powers. These individuals manipulate the human desire for something extraordinary, exploiting people's vulnerabilities and gullibility for personal gain. The examples provided shed light on some common tricks used by charlatans to fool people into believing in their supposed supernatural abilities.

Cold Reading: Cold reading is a technique used by many pretenders claiming to have psychic or clairvoyant powers. By using vague statements and carefully observing verbal and non-verbal cues, these fraudsters can make seemingly accurate guesses or provide general information that appears specific to an individual. For instance, they might say, "I sense a loved one who has passed away is watching over you. They had a name that starts with the letter 'J'?" The person being read might then fill in the details themselves, believing the cold reader has divine insight.

Sleight of Hand: Performers may employ various sleight-of-hand techniques to create illusions of magical or supernatural powers. They might claim to make objects disappear, reappear, or change form using quick hand movements, distractions, and misdirection. These tricks rely on the audience's limited perception and the skillful manipulation of their attention. For instance, a phony might pretend to levitate a small object, using invisible threads or magnets to give the illusion of defying gravity.

Prop Manipulation: Another trick employed by charlatans involves the use of specially designed props to create the illusion of supernatural power. These props can range from simple mechanical contraptions to intricate devices. For example, a trickster might present a "magic" crystal ball that appears to reveal hidden knowledge or a mystical artifact that purportedly possesses healing properties. These objects are often cleverly crafted to produce specific effects, creating an air of mystique around the charlatan.

Psychological Manipulation: Grifters often exploit psychological techniques to manipulate their audience's beliefs and emotions. They may use tactics such as cold reading, group dynamics, or playing on people's fears and desires to establish a sense of authority and trust. By creating a carefully orchestrated atmosphere, they make it easier for individuals to suspend their disbelief and accept the charlatan's claims.

Prearranged "Miracles": Some hustlers orchestrate elaborate scenarios to create the illusion of performing miracles or supernatural events. For example, they might collaborate with confederates who pretend to be healed or possessed, thereby convincing the audience of their divine powers. These staged events can include fake healings, prophecies, or even claiming to communicate with spirits or supernatural entities.

It's important to note that these tricks are not indicative of genuine supernatural abilities. Frauds exploit the human inclination to seek something extraordinary, often causing harm and financial loss to those who place their trust in them. It is crucial to approach claims of magical or divine power with skepticism and critical thinking, as these deceptions can prey on vulnerable individuals and exploit their beliefs for personal gain.

Chapter Seventeen – The Wisdom of Wizards

In the realm of fantasy, the word "wizard" often conjures images of bearded figures casting spells and wielding magical powers. However, the true essence of a wizard goes far beyond these fantastical portrayals. At its core, the term "wizard" stems from the Old English word "wīsġerē," meaning "wise one." And indeed, wizards were historically revered as the embodiment of wisdom, embodying the ideals of philosophers, scientists, researchers, and mystics.

Throughout the ages, wizards delved into the secrets of the universe that were available to them at the time. They dedicated their lives to seeking answers to all of life's questions, exploring the intricacies of existence, and uncovering the hidden forces that govern our world. Rather than relying solely on supernatural abilities, wizards relied on their intellect, knowledge, and unquenchable curiosity to unravel the mysteries of the cosmos.

Being a wizard, therefore, is not limited to the possession of innate magical powers. Instead, it is an ardent pursuit of wisdom and understanding. It is a lifelong commitment to learning and exploring the world around us, driven by a deep-seated curiosity that propels us forward.

A true wizard is a polymath, someone who seeks to acquire knowledge in various domains. They understand that wisdom does not reside solely within the confines of a single discipline. Instead, they embrace the vast spectrum of human understanding, delving into the sciences, mathematics, languages, cultures, religion, geography, medicine, and much more.

In their pursuit of wisdom, wizards embark on a continuous journey of self-improvement. They recognize that knowledge is a boundless ocean, and they strive to expand their understanding with each passing day. They immerse themselves in the great works of philosophers, engaging in intellectual discourse and contemplation. They experiment with scientific principles, pushing the boundaries of human understanding. They study languages to bridge the gaps between cultures, fostering empathy and appreciation for diverse perspectives. They explore the intricacies of religions, seeking spiritual enlightenment and connection with the universe. They delve into geography, understanding the world's landscapes and the interconnectedness of all beings. They investigate the mysteries of medicine, striving to alleviate suffering and promote well-being.

To be a wizard, one must cultivate a sense of wonder and maintain an insatiable appetite for knowledge. They understand that true wisdom lies not in claiming to possess all answers but in recognizing the vastness of the unknown. It is through embracing this humility that they open themselves to new possibilities, unearthing insights that lead to profound discoveries.

The path of a wizard is not without challenges. It requires discipline, dedication, and an unwavering commitment to intellectual growth. But with each step taken, the wizard inches closer to enlightenment, unraveling the intricacies of the universe and gaining a deeper understanding of the self.

The essence of being a wizard lies in the pursuit of wisdom. Wizards are not mere conjurers of magic; they are seekers of truth and understanding. By cultivating a thirst for knowledge and embracing a multidisciplinary approach, they unlock the secrets of the world. So, let us embark on this journey together, for within each of us lies the potential to become a wise one—a wizard in our own right.

Chapter Eighteen – Setting Up Shop

In some towns and villages, the presence of a local wizard or wise person can add a touch of magic and mystique to the community. These individuals are often seen as the go-to experts when it comes to solving complex or unusual problems that require a touch of supernatural or mystical intervention. While wizards are mostly associated with folklore and fantasy, there are instances where real-life individuals have embraced the persona of a wizard to provide assistance and guidance to their communities.

For example, in New Zealand, there is a town called Christchurch that gained fame for having its very own wizard. Ian Brackenbury Channell, commonly known as "The Wizard," became an iconic figure in the city. He began performing as a wizard in the late 1970s, offering his wisdom, wit, and eccentricity to the residents and visitors of Christchurch. The Wizard became a beloved and recognizable figure, providing a sense of wonder and enchantment to the community.

Ian Brackenbury Channell, is a street performer and self-proclaimed wizard who has become synonymous with Christchurch's identity. Born in 1932 in New South Wales, Australia, Channell moved to New Zealand in the 1970s and began his magical journey.

Channell started his career as a lecturer in sociology at the University of New South Wales. However, he felt disillusioned with academia and decided to pursue his passion for magic and wizardry. In 1974, he arrived in Christchurch and began performing on the streets, captivating audiences with his eccentric persona, philosophical musings, and magical tricks.

The Wizard's performances often involve a combination of humor, satire, and thought-provoking ideas. He can be seen wearing a long robe, a pointed hat, and carrying a staff as he engages with passersby. Channell delivers improvised speeches on a variety of topics, from politics and philosophy to spirituality and the environment. He has a unique ability to blend entertainment and intellectual discourse, attracting locals and tourists alike.

Beyond his street performances, the Wizard has played a significant role in the civic life of Christchurch. He became involved in local politics and actively participated in public debates and discussions, offering his unconventional viewpoints. He has often advocated for preserving the city's heritage, protecting the environment, and fostering creativity and free thinking.

Channell's dedication to Christchurch and his contributions to the city led to his appointment as the official Wizard of New Zealand by the Prime Minister in 1990, a role he held until 2018. Although the position holds no official power, it symbolizes the city's recognition of his unique cultural significance.

As for other towns with their own wizards, while it is rare to find individuals like the Wizard of Christchurch, some places have embraced the idea of a resident wizard or magical figure. For example, the city of Wollongong in Australia had a local wizard named Amethyst Realm who gained attention in the 1990s. In addition, the city of Wellington in New Zealand had a street performer known as The Wellington Wizard, although he retired in 2013. These figures, like the Wizard of Christchurch, added a touch of whimsy and enchantment to their respective cities.

The types of situations in which a wizard or wise person can provide assistance vary greatly and often depend on the specific beliefs and traditions associated with the wizard's role. Here are some examples of the sorts of things a wizard could help with:

Enigmatic dilemmas: Wizards can offer their wisdom and perspective on complex personal or community issues, helping individuals see things from different angles and find creative solutions.

Magical storytelling: Wizards have a knack for spinning tales that captivate and inspire. They can entertain and educate through storytelling, imparting wisdom and life lessons to their audience.

Spiritual guidance: People seeking spiritual insight or guidance beyond traditional religious channels may turn to a wizard for alternative perspectives and spiritual practices.

Divination and prophecy: Wizards might offer insights into the future, providing predictions or guidance on matters such as relationships, career choices, or upcoming events.

Magical protection and warding: Wizards can create spells or rituals to protect against negative energy, ward off evil spirits, or bring good luck to individuals or places.

Healing and herbal remedies: Some wizards possess knowledge of ancient herbal remedies and alternative healing methods, providing treatments for ailments or offering advice on maintaining well-being.

Spellcasting and enchantments: Wizards may specialize in casting spells or creating magical artifacts to bring about desired outcomes, such as attracting love, improving prosperity, or resolving conflicts.

Rituals and ceremonies: Wizards can officiate ceremonies and rituals for significant life events, including weddings, funerals, blessings, naming ceremonies, or community events, infusing them with a touch of mysticism and adding an element of humor or enchantment.

To set up shop as a wizard in a small town, there are certain items and characteristics that can enhance the wizard's aura of quirkiness and mystery. While these may not be necessary, they contribute to the theatrical and enchanting experience for those seeking their help. Some examples include:

Quirky attire: A distinctive robe, hat, or cape can help create an aura of mystery and enchantment around the wizard. Darker robes of indigo might be just the thing, with silvery moons and stars embroidered in them, or a lighter-colored kaftan. Whatever it is, make sure that it is obvious to all that you are a wizard and are here to do wizard stuff.

Staff or wand: A staff or wand can be used as a symbolic prop during rituals, ceremonies, or simply as a visual representation of the wizard's power and wisdom.

Books of knowledge: A collection of books on diverse subjects, including mythology, folklore, philosophy, and the occult, can lend an air of erudition and expertise to the wizard.

Alchemical tools: Assorted vials, jars, and esoteric artifacts can be displayed as props, hinting at the wizard's mastery over hidden knowledge.

Business card or flyer: A unique and creatively designed business card or flyer can serve as a memorable keepsake for those who seek the wizard's assistance, adding to the overall experience.

It's important to note that the role of a wizard in a community is more about providing an imaginative and unconventional perspective rather than performing actual magical feats. Their allure lies in the aura of mystery they cultivate and the unique insights they offer, adding a touch of enchantment and wonder to the lives of those who seek their counsel.

A wizard's shop is a place of enchantment and wonder, where mystical artifacts, magical ingredients, and arcane knowledge come together. The appearance of a wizard's shop can vary, reflecting the unique personality and tastes of the individual wizard who owns it. Here are a few examples of what a wizard's shop might look like, each offering a different ambiance and experience:

The Enchanted Emporium: This wizard's shop is a whimsical and fantastical place, resembling a cross between a dusty old bookshop and an apothecary. The shelves are filled with ancient tomes and spellbooks, while glass jars containing various enchanted items line the countertops. The shop is dimly lit, and soft, flickering candles cast dancing shadows on the walls. A slight scent of incense lingers in the air, and mystical symbols are etched on the wooden floors. Customers might stumble upon hidden nooks and crannies, uncovering mysterious artifacts and magical trinkets.

The Wizard's Brew: This wizard's shop is a whimsical and enchanting place, often located in a quaint part of town. The exterior might feature a vibrant color scheme, with intricate carvings and mystical symbols adorning the walls. Inside, the shop is filled with sparkling crystals, colorful potions, and magical trinkets suspended from the ceiling. The atmosphere is warm and inviting, with soft music playing and a cozy fireplace crackling in the corner.

Arcane Alcove: Tucked away in a hidden alley, this wizard's shop exudes an air of mystery and intrigue. The exterior is more subdued, with a weathered wooden sign that creaks softly in the wind. Inside, the shop is dimly lit by flickering candlelight, casting eerie shadows on shelves lined with ancient spell books and arcane artifacts. Mysterious symbols are etched into the floor, and a velvet curtain separates the backroom where the most powerful and rare magical items are kept.

Elemental Boutique: This wizard's shop specializes in elemental magic and is often located near natural landmarks such as a forest or a river. The shop might have a rustic exterior, blending in with its surroundings, and a small garden of herbs and mystical plants at the entrance. Inside, the atmosphere is filled with the scent of herbs and flowers, and the walls are adorned with tapestries depicting the elements. Each section of the shop represents a different element, with bubbling cauldrons for water magic, flickering torches for fire magic, and wind chimes for air magic.

Timeless Treasures: Housed in a centuries-old building, this wizard's shop is a treasure trove of artifacts and ancient knowledge. The exterior has an antique charm, with ivy-covered walls and a wrought-iron gate. Inside, the shop is filled with dusty tomes, intricate maps, and magical relics from forgotten times. The air is tinged with a hint of ancient magic, and the shopkeeper is often an elderly wizard who possesses vast wisdom and tales of bygone eras.

It's important to note that these are just a few examples, and the appearance of a wizard's shop will very much depend on the individual. Feel free to let your creative energies go and make the space for your own place of magic. Hopefully, this book has given you some ideas about how to become a wizard. The rest is up to your own curiosity, research, and hard work. It is a lifelong journey of discovery. Good luck.

Afterword:

We hope you have enjoyed Whispers of the Arcane: A Journey into the World of Wizards. This is the first book in Norman Creek Press's 'Journey into the World of' series. Future installments will be available soon. If you have enjoyed this story, please review it on Amazon and Good Reads. You can also check out our social media below.

Norman Creek Press Independent Publishers

Norman Creek Press is an independent publisher of science fiction, horror, and fantasy fiction. We also produce low-content stationery, coloring books, and other titles. Check out our social media below for more information.

Amazon: https://www.amazon.com.au/Norman-Creek-Press/e/B09CV4SYN7

Twitter: https://twitter.com/Norman_Creek_Px

Pinterest: https://www.pinterest.com.au/normancreekpress/

Instagram: https://www.instagram.com/normancreekpress/

Facebook Business Page: https://www.facebook.com/NormanCreekPress

Webpage: Normancreekpress.com

Ko-fi: https://ko-fi.com/normancreekpress

Printed in Great Britain
by Amazon